MOUNTAIN BIKE
MASTER

MOUNTAIN BIKE MASTER

Essential SKILLS and Advanced TECHNIQUES Made Easy

Mark Langton

MENASHA RIDGE PRESS
www.menasharidge.com

DISCLAIMER

The information in this book is provided for educational purposes only. Mountain biking is a potentially dangerous sport, and the reader accepts a number of inherent and unavoidable risks. Practicing and performing the techniques described in this book in no way guarantees the safety of the rider or any property while riding a mountain bike. Always make sure your equipment is in good working order, and wear appropriate safety gear. While substantial effort has been made to provide accurate information, neither Mark Langton nor Menasha Ridge Press accepts liability for any errors or omissions, or for any injuries or losses incurred from using this book.

Copyright © 2008 by Mark Langton

Published by Menasha Ridge Press
Printed in the United States of America
Distributed by Publishers Group West
First edition, first printing

Text and cover design by Travis Bryant
Cover and interior photographs by Kash Dadvand

Library of Congress Cataloging-in-Publication Data

Langton, Mark.
   Mountain bike master: essential skills and advanced techniques made easy/by Mark Langton. —1st ed.
      p. cm.
   ISBN-13: 978-0-89732-435-9
   ISBN-10: 0-89732-435-8
   1. All-terrain cycling. I. Title.

GV1056L364 2008
796.63—dc22

                                            2007026198

Menasha Ridge Press
P.O. Box 43673
Birmingham, Alabama 35243
www.menasharidge.com

Table of Contents

Introduction

Mountain biking, like most sports, requires biomechanical techniques. In other words, proper fundamental skills are needed to become more proficient. Some skills, however, require more trust and less analysis. For example, most people are afraid of being pitched forward over the handlebar on a steep hill, so they straighten and tense their arms, thinking that locking hard to the handlebar will keep them from being pitched forward. Actually, the opposite is true. You must relax, bending your arms and your waist while moving your weight rearward, putting your upper body (and head) closer to the handlebar. Putting yourself closer to the handlebar and therefore closer to the front wheel might seem counterintuitive, but often you need to turn off your brain and trust your technique to become a truly advanced rider. Because fear responses often paralyze your body, I tell riders that the brain is probably the biggest obstacle to becoming a better biker. If you can replace the fear with technique, then you can focus on the mechanics. It's sort of like having a mantra: tell yourself to relax, and you'll relax. Sounds simplistic, but it works.

Even the most talented and successful athletes practice the fundamentals regularly. In the case of professional athletes, this means repetition and review from a coach or trainer. But most of us can't afford a coach, so we must first learn the basics and then practice, practice, practice. When you're out on the trail, pay close attention to what you're doing at all times. If you have trouble with a section of terrain, ride through it several times until you feel comfortable with your technique. This book will help you understand and perform the fundamentals, and enable you to learn more-advanced riding techniques. But you must build on the basics first, creating a sound foundation of proper technique so you can reach the next level.

After 25 years of riding mountain bikes and 20 years of coaching riders—from beginners to experts—I still learn things that I can improve on, and that's why I love this sport so much: it's always a challenge, and it never gets boring. Whether you've been riding for a long time or you're just starting out, I encourage you to master the fundamentals in this book before moving on to the advanced skills. Your patience will be rewarded by more confident and controlled riding in all types of terrain.

Yours in dirt,
Mark Langton

1

1 Fundamentals

RIDER COMPARTMENT

The lines between the pedals, saddle, and handlebar delineate the rider compartment.
Five components determine the dimensions of the compartment: (1) saddle angle;
(2) frame size; (3) seat height/leg extension; (4) handlebar height and reach; and
(5) brake-lever angle.

Saddle Angle

Before making any adjustments to the rider compartment, make sure the saddle
is level, with the rear and front parallel to the ground. Also, the saddle should be
clamped at the midway point along the rails (see figure 1.1).

Frame Size

When you straddle the bike just in front of the saddle, there should be four to six inches between the top tube of the bike and your crotch. When you purchase a bike, take
advantage of the shop's knowledge in regard to choosing the best frame size. Frame
sizing has become quite sophisticated over the years. Mountain bikes with severely
sloping top tubes and the advent of female-specific geometries are two examples.

Seat Height/Leg Extension

Correct seat height enables proper leg extension for maximum power delivery. A low
saddle may feel safer to new mountain bikers because they can reach the ground more

**Generally, the seat post should be clamping the saddle at about the middle of the
saddle rails (silver horizontal tubes).**

1.1

Correct saddle height: you should barely be able to touch the ground with your toe.

easily. However, sitting too low compromises the leg's efficiency by limiting extension. Unlike on a road bike, where you have an exact formula for determining leg extension, on a mountain bike it can be a little more loosely interpreted.

First, raise the saddle so that when you sit on the bike, you can rest your feet flat on the ground. Make sure your "sit points" (the ischial tuberosities of the pelvic-bone structure) are resting on the wider rear portion of the saddle, not toward the middle. Next, dismount and raise the saddle about four inches so that you can put one foot on one pedal and the other on the ground while sitting on the saddle. Note the position of the foot that is touching the ground: if you are touching the ground with your heel raised and the ball of your foot on the

Proper leg extension at bottom of pedal revolution

Proper leg position at top of pedal revolution

ground, dismount and raise the saddle another couple of inches, and then remount. The goal is to have the saddle high enough that you can only touch the ground with the tips of the toes, with ankles flexed and toes pointing downward. You may want to position your bike next to a curb so you can support yourself with one foot on the curb while you check the position of the other foot relative to the ground (see figure 1.2).

Once you've fixed the saddle height to where your toes touch the ground while seated, place one foot on the ground (preferably a curb) and place the other foot on the pedal. Rotate the foot on the pedal to 6 o'clock, and note the bend in

A telltale sign that the saddle is too low is excessive knee bend and the heel dropping below the pedal at the bottom of the revolution.

the knee. It should have a bend at an angle of about 40 degrees (see figure 1.3). If there is a tight feeling at the back of the knee, the saddle is too high. Another way to check this is to rotate the foot that is on the pedal to 12 o'clock and note the position of the knee and thigh; the knee should be slightly lower than the hip (see figure 1.4). If the knee is even with or higher than the hip, the saddle is too low. Once you have the saddle height in the proper position, pedal around an area that is free from traffic and obstacles. It's best to have someone watch you and look for two things:

1) Heel position at the bottom of the pedal stroke—if your heel is below the ball of the foot at the bottom of the pedal stroke (6 o'clock), the saddle needs to come up about a half inch (see figure 1.5).

2) Hips at the top and bottom of the pedal stroke—while watching from behind while riding, note your hip position. If your hips appear to push upward at the top of the pedal stroke, the saddle should be raised by about a half inch; if your hips seem to dip downward at the bottom of the pedal stroke, the saddle should be lowered by about a half inch.

Handlebar Height and Reach

The handlebar's height and reach are determined by the saddle height. Once the saddle has been raised to approximately the correct height for your personal leg extension, the handlebar should be positioned at, but no more than, two inches below the saddle height (see figure 1.6). If the handlebar is above the saddle height, assuming the desired positions for climbing and descending becomes awkward. A handlebar height that is higher than the saddle feels comfortable on a level bike path, but is not useful for riding in the dirt. Mountain biking requires a body position that allows you to bend your upper body down toward the bike so your arms bend comfortably to control steering and proper weight distribution. A handlebar position that is too high makes your arms feel confined, inducing you to sit up to feel more comfortable. Sitting upright places the body in an unbalanced position, making the bike top-heavy and unstable.

The handlebar's reach, or lateral distance from the head tube, should be such that there is a comfortable bend in the arms when seated. If your arms have more than a 70-degree bend while sitting on the bike, the reach is too short. If your arms are nearly straight, the reach is too long. A general test is to sit on the bike and look down at the handlebar, noting where the front wheel's hub appears as you look down at it. You should not be able to see the front hub; the handlebar should obscure the hub. If the hub appears to be in front of the handlebar, the stem may be too short. If the hub appears to be behind the handlebar, the stem may be too long.

When saddle is at correct height for proper leg extension, handlebar height should be at or slightly below saddle height.

1.6

Brake-lever Angle

Once you have dialed in the rider compartment, position the brake levers at an angle that puts the hands and forearms relatively in line with each other. Do not angle the brake levers at 90 degrees (parallel with the ground)—they should be angled downward at approximately 35 degrees. This keeps the muscles of the hands and forearms in line so that you are maximizing the braking power from those groups of muscles. When the brake levers parallel the ground, typically only the muscles in the fingers supply power because the wrists are rotated downward (see figures 1.7 and 1.8).

GENERAL SEATED-RIDING POSITION

Although sitting on the bike and riding may seem like simple procedures, they too require basic skills to enhance stability and control.

A mountain bike loaded with a rider is extremely top-heavy. To stabilize the bike, relax and bend your elbows and waist to lower your center of gravity.

Dirt changes the whole way you ride, including how you negotiate turns and small variances in the terrain. Mountain biking requires you to be much more nimble aboard the bike. Because of small rocks, ruts, and other things that can send you in a different direction quickly, the seated-riding position is actually very important, much more so than when riding on the road. Even though you sit on

the saddle the same way as on a road bike, it is more important that you be aware of this position on a mountain bike because it allows you to ride from your core (your abdominal and back muscles). When the correct saddle position is combined with the upper-body position described on the following pages, the bike doesn't react as severely to an unexpected directional change because your body isn't affecting the direction it's going as much. You should be sitting on the wider rear portion of the saddle, sometimes called the wings, with your sit points contacting the saddle rather than your perineum (the soft-tissue area of your crotch).

If you sit toward the middle of the saddle, putting pressure on your

Brake levers should be angled downward for better braking power and control.

1.7

perineum instead of the sit points, you'll be uncomfortable and less balanced than you could be. A word to the wise: riding on your crotch is the primary cause of numbness in the genital area. To relieve numbness, adjust your position rearward on the saddle to the sit points, and raise off the saddle periodically to increase blood flow to the area. Padded bike shorts can also help to alleviate saddle numbness, but the correct position and occasionally raising off the saddle are the best medicine.

Overly padded saddles may be comfortable when you first sit on them, but in the long run they will not promote comfort. In fact, they can actually increase the possibility of numbness as the perineum sinks down into the padding, putting pressure on nerves and arteries. It comes down to getting the body used to sitting on the saddle correctly. A saddle that has a minimal amount of padding and a channel running down the center is a much better choice.

As for the loftier parts of your body, your torso compensates for sudden changes in the bike's attitude—that is, the way the bike leans as it reacts to a directional change. To do this effectively, your upper body must be supported from the core, the hips (ischial tuberosities), stomach, and lower-back muscles. If you support your upper body primarily by leaning on the handlebar with straight arms (see figure 1.9), your arms will be

Incorrect lever position

1.8

rigid and unable to react to even small changes in the terrain or the bike's direction. Your arms should be relaxed and slightly bent. As you ride, you can test if your arms are relaxed; flap your arms as if trying to touch your elbows to your sides. You will feel the stomach and back muscles come into play more. Make sure you keep your elbows lowered, not pointed out (see figure 1.10).

Your hands and wrists also play a big part in proper riding posture. Your hands should rest with the base of the thumb on the handlebar, not the heel of the hand. To be specific, the V at the base of the forefinger and the thumb is what should be resting on the handlebar grip. Make sure your wrists are not rotated downward; this will cause your arms to tense up. Rotate your wrists upward so that they are relatively in line with the forearms.

Be conscious of your shoulders; do not hunch them, and check to see if they are relaxed (take a deep breath and forcibly exhale). Also, do not arch your back. Instead, you should have a slightly rounded shape to your back (see figure 1.10).

To test that you are supporting yourself with your core while riding, bend your waist and arms, and move your shoulders toward either side of the bike (see figure 1.11) so that your head is over your hand on each side. This will allow you to be more nimble and react to the bike changing direction quickly.

Incorrect seated-riding position: body upright and forward on the saddle, arms straight, shoulders hunched, arms leaning on the handlebar, wrists rotated downward

SHIFTING

Mountain bikes offer a wide range of gear selections. Matching up a front chainring with a rear cog creates a specific gear ratio. You can easily shift into any given gear ratio, but the trick is to match the gear ratio with the terrain and your power output. Staying in the same gear while riding from flat terrain onto an upward slope slows you down, creates leg strain, and stresses the bike's drivetrain. As the terrain shifts, shift gears.

If you are unfamiliar with your bike's shifting system, place the bike in a stand (ask your local bike shop to assist you), pedal, and engage the gear shifters while watching how the chain moves up and down the chainrings.

A mountain bike drivetrain consists of two sets of gears (front and back), two derailleurs (front and back), the chain, the crank arms, and the crank spindle (the shaft connecting the crank arms). Feet pressing and pulling on the pedals turn the crank arms, which turn the crank spindle. The cranks spin the front set of gears, driving the chain forward and delivering power to the rear wheel through the rear set of cogs.

Mountain bikes have three gear ranges that are determined by the front set of chainrings. Pairing one of the three front rings with a rear cog creates a gear ratio. Range one (front inner chainring) requires the least power to maintain a steady cadence (revolutions

Correct seated-riding position: body slightly lowered, arms and shoulders slightly bent and relaxed, body supported with core muscles, sit points situated on wide rear part of the saddle

1.10

per minute) on level ground and makes climbing hills easy. Biking down a hill in range one results in spinning pedals that contribute nothing to momentum. Range two (front-middle chainring) covers the middle ground and is best for flat and gently rolling terrain. Range three (large outer chainring) requires the most power to maintain a given cadence on flat ground but makes accelerating down hills possible. Biking up a hill in range three makes for slow, difficult pedaling.

Pairing a front ring with the best-choice gear on your rear set of chainrings allows you to fine-tune your cadence, making pedaling easier

Bending your waist and relaxing you arms while moving your head over each hand helps develop balance and maneuverability.

1.11

or more difficult. Shift front and rear gears often to help you find that perfect cadence for the terrain and your power output.

Ideally, you should change gears with a minimum amount of stress on the drivetrain, especially when going from level ground to a slope. Do this by shifting into an easier gear before you begin climbing a hill, rather than when you are already on the hill and pushing hard on the pedals. If you need to shift into an easier gear while pushing hard on the pedals, let up on the power (but keep pedaling) just before you shift, and wait for the chain to move to the next gear before putting the power back on.

When you have momentum going into a hill—for instance, when moving from a downhill to an uphill—you should shift into an easier gear just as you begin climbing, even though it feels like you have a lot of momentum to carry you up the hill. This should become automatic; as soon as you begin climbing, shift into one or two easier gears, no matter how much momentum you have.

You'll want to keep the same cadence going up as you had coming down. When transitioning quickly from a downhill to an uphill and there is very little pressure from your pedals, you need to slow your cadence down and let the bike slow down until your gear ratio matches the speed of your bike. Do not try to pedal as fast as you can to try to match the cadence with the gear ratio and hill, or you will more than likely lose your balance.

Shifting the chain on the front chainrings takes a bit of finesse, especially if you want to change the chain from the middle to the small chainring when climbing. You should always let up slightly on the power as you shift the chain on the chainrings in either direction. However, when you are already on a hill and need to shift from the middle to the small chainring and there is a lot of pressure on the pedals, you must accelerate first for one or two revolutions, then back off the power just as you shift the front derailleur. During this process, the bike will slow down as the chain drops to the small chainring. Keep the pedals going around for about one-half to three-quarters of a pedal revolution (see figures 1.12 and 1.13) until the chain drops, then resume full power.

BASIC BRAKING

Braking technique on a bicycle is much like a car or motorcycle: you should do most of your braking prior to the turn, avoiding any heavy braking while the bike is leaning. As you approach a turn, use your brakes to scrub off speed so that you can ride through the corner comfortably without applying the brakes. Keep your fingers out on the levers just in case you need to reapply the brakes, and if you do need to apply them while in a turn, keep your chest low and arms bent, and look into the turn.

If you felt as if there were a giant magnet at the outside of the turn, you more than likely went into it with too much speed and probably felt the need to brake in the turn. When you apply the brakes in a turn, you arrest the wheels' (not the bike's) centrifugal force, which makes the bike stand out of its lean, go straight, and head toward that invisible magnet. Keeping your chest low and eyes trained into the turn creates stability and moves the bike in the right direction. Remember to look where you want to go—toward the inside of the turn, not where you *don't* want to go—toward the outside of the turn.

Fundamentally, you should always apply both brakes at the same time. Braking technique changes, though, as terrain steepens and becomes increasingly technical. (See page 52 for more details on advanced braking techniques.) Many riders think that applying too much front brake will pitch them over the handlebar. Maintaining correct body position while braking makes this

Shifting from middle to small chainring: It takes about a half a pedal revolution for the chain to drop from the middle to the small ring. Reduce power while shifting to facilitate a smooth shift.

situation very unlikely (see the Crouch, figure 1.16).

I've had students tell me that they've been told to stay off the front brake in some downhill situations. I disagree and think that using less front brake can actually be dangerous. Because your body's and the bike's weight are behind the front brake, it has more stopping power in relation to momentum. By using less front brake than rear brake, bikers limit their brakes' effectiveness. So learn to trust the front brake while employing proper body position.

With today's powerful braking systems, a single finger is often sufficient for braking. For most scenarios, I recommend using the middle finger (figure 1.14). This allows you to grip the handlebar with four fingers, especially the index finger and thumb, which gives you a greater degree of control. If you need extra power, you can also use your index finger as well as your middle finger (see figure 1.15). Keep in mind, however, that while braking your grip will be more on the brake lever than the handlebar, which sometimes results in overbraking.

CADENCE

Cadence is the rhythm of the spinning pedals. A slow cadence results in lower pedal revolutions per minute (rpm); a fast cadence yields higher rpm. Monitoring cadence is extremely important for efficient

Using only the middle finger while braking allows you to use the thumb and index finger for a stronger grip.

Two-finger braking can cause excessive power and possible overbraking.

power delivery and management of forward motion. Because you are the motor, you determine the cadence, but you must also match cadence and gear selection to your power output and the terrain.

Flat terrain requires the least effort at maintaining cadence. Rolling terrain with slight rises and descents (middle chainring range) is not as critical for paying close attention to cadence. The general rule of thumb is to be pedaling at a cadence of between 60 and 80 rpm. As you ascend, shift the bike early (see pages 11–13) into one or two easier gear positions in the rear, even though you may not need the easier ratio until farther up the hill. This allows your legs to spin smoothly through the transition to the uphill, effectively reducing strain and saving strength.

When the hills get steeper and longer, you should be pedaling at a cadence that allows you to keep your rpm up, even if you hit a slight rise or bump that slows your momentum. Often I see mountain bikers try to keep their bikes in a gear that gives them a lot of pressure from the pedals because it makes them feel more stable (they don't want to pedal at high/easy rpm because they are unsure of their balance). However, pedaling at a higher/easier cadence keeps your legs turning more quickly, preventing a bog-down should you suddenly decelerate. No need to spin like a propeller, though; always pedal in a gear and at a speed that is comfortable and feels as if there is some pressure coming up into your bike shoes.

Of course, some hills are so steep that it is very difficult to pedal even in

DISC BRAKES VERSUS CANTILEVERS The debate continues regarding whether disc brakes are necessary. Riders in Washington and Maine will give you a resounding yes. But ask those in the Southwest, and you'll more likely get "What for?" than an affirmative response. Several factors (not all of them related to wet riding conditions) make disc brakes desirable. With today's lightweight systems, disc brakes weigh scant grams—if any—more than cantilevers. Also, consider that in most cases disc brakes are more powerful than cantilevers, giving you better overall control. One could argue that if something gives you more control, then it's a necessity (this is the argument I use all the time for rear suspension). However, the true answer to the question "Do you *need* disc brakes?" is no. That being said, I would no sooner go back to riding a bike without rear suspension than I would go back to cantilever brakes, given a disc brake's superior stopping power and modulation, resistance to fade, and overall performance in wet or dry conditions. And of course, if you crash and tweak your rim out of alignment, disc brakes still work. In most cases, the only way a bent rim will roll through a cantilever brake is by adjusting the brake to a position that makes it virtually useless.

your easiest gear. Making it up these hills is dependent on several factors, including traction and climbing technique (not to mention conditioning), which I will discuss in the section on climbing on the following pages. But for now, just remember to shift early into an easy gear, before the pressure needed to push down on the pedals creates an undue strain.

SCANNING

Scanning simply means paying attention. Mountain biking is an extremely cerebral sport. In other words, you should never fully relax while riding in the dirt; there are too many things that can surprise you. One of the best things you can do to stay focused is to always look where you want to be going. This means that if you see something on the trail you don't want to ride over, don't continue to stare at it. Recognize the obstacle, then look for the desired line around (or over) it.

The faster you go, the farther ahead you should be looking. I like to think of it as trying to prepare for your next two moves. Playing this game in your head will train you to scan into the distance, bring your sight line back to a few feet ahead, and then back into the distance. Repeat.

BASIC CORNERING

The initiation of a turn should always begin with a shift of the upper body downward toward the top tube, so remember to keep your arms relaxed so

that you can make this movement. This helps lower your body's center of gravity and keep the bike more stable.

When cornering, you should practice looking into the turn, not just with your eyes but also by turning your head. Look into the turn as if you were looking for another rider, hiker, or equestrian coming toward you.

Braking should always be done prior to fully leaning into the turn.

Putting on the brakes forces the bike to go upright, which then makes the bike go straight, so it's difficult to turn the bike when the brakes are applied. Also, if you apply the brakes in a turn, you run the risk of the front tire skidding out as the bike leans.

Practice cornering and braking by first turning on a solid surface (pavement); pick a spot where you can make a relaxed 90-degree turn. As you approach the turn, look into the turn, apply the brakes, drop your body into the bike, and then as you lean the bike over, release the brakes and continue looking into the turn until it's completed.

CLIMBING (SEATED)

Climbing hills on a mountain bike is a necessary evil, but there's no other way to enjoy the downhills!

The most efficient way to climb is when seated on the saddle. This position keeps your body correctly balanced. Several components to climbing, however, need to be considered.

LOOKING INTO THE TURN

Any time you begin a turn while seated, you should drop your chest (bend your waist and arms) so that the bike becomes more stable. Always initiate a turn by looking into it and dropping your chest. You should never focus on the front tire. Always look where you want to go, not where you don't want to go. If you focus on an obstacle or where you don't want to go, you *will* go there!

STEP ONE

Much as with descending, when climbing you have to position yourself on the bike to compensate for the variance in weight transference. For climbing, this means relaxing your arms and sliding forward, toward the middle of the saddle, while remaining seated and moving your upper body downward toward the bike.

STEP TWO

Most of the time your legs have plenty of power to get you up a hill. But there are times when you need extra power—even when you're in the easiest gear—that can come only from your upper body.

If you've ever experienced the bike weaving back and forth across the trail or the front tire popping up with each pedal stroke, it's probably because you're pulling up on the handlebar. The solution is to move your body down into the bike while pulling down on the handlebar with each pedal stroke. It's much like a rowing motion, but you are actually pulling down on and releasing the handlebar every time you push down on the pedal. This will counteract the twisting motion in the upper body created by your legs as they push down on the pedals. Pulling down also keeps your shoulders square to the handlebar, a position that will help you go straighter up the trail.

There are two other effective biome-chanical climbing techniques that involve the upper body. The first is to rotate the wrists upward slightly to get a better pulling angle on the handlebar. The second is to bring your elbows inward with each tug on the handlebar. Think of it as trying to squeeze against a tennis ball that's under your armpit every time the pedal comes around while pulling on the handlebar.

Keep your arms relaxed as you pull on the handlebar. If you lock your elbows, it's the same as pulling up on the bar, and the end results are the same: the front tire comes up off the ground or twists from side to side.

DESCENDING/ TECHNICAL TERRAIN

What I call "the Crouch" is the most important all-around position for dealing with rough terrain, especially while descending. It's somewhat like the athletic position in sports—feet apart, knees bent, waist bent, balancing on the balls of your feet. For riding downhill and/or negotiating obstacles with momentum, picture a jockey aboard a galloping horse. Here are the steps (also see figure 1.16):

- While coasting, put the pedals level and stand up, extending your legs so that you have a gap between your rear and the saddle.

Seated-climbing position: Slide forward on the saddle, lower upper body while keeping arms relaxed, and pull downward and rearward on the handlebar with each pedal stroke.

- Make sure the pressure is even on both pedals and that you feel as though you're bouncing slightly on the balls of your feet, much like an athletic "ready position."

- Your knees should be slightly bent, and your waist should be bent so that the insides of your thighs (not your rear) are contacting the saddle.

- Arms should be bent and firm but relaxed—do not push your weight back to the rear of the saddle by straightening your arms. Bent arms give you maneuverability for steering changes and allow the front tire to track over bumps.

- Weight should be balanced on the feet, with very little pressure leaning on the handlebar.

- Always cover your brake levers while in the Crouch (one or two fingers, index and/or middle) so that you're ready for braking. This will reduce reaction time if you have to brake quickly.

- Do not arch your back. Instead, your back should have a slight hunch or rounded shape to it.

- Keep your head up and your eyes focused down the trail.

The Crouch position does two things. First, it allows you to ride weightlessly, letting the bike roll over rough terrain without your body counteracting the natural motion of the bike's wheels. Second, it redistributes your weight so that when you brake, your weight does not pitch out in front of the bike. Keeping your weight low and to the rear enhances stability and braking.

Remember to let your arms bend as the front tire goes over an obstacle. The faster you're going or the steeper the hill, the more you need to bend your

CORE CONSIDERATIONS Your back and abdominal muscles, aka your core, support the majority of your upper body's weight, but it's important for your back to be not only strong but flexible as well. Plenty of exercise books can show you ways to strengthen your core muscles; still, there's no better exercise to strengthen your abs than crunch sit-ups. Lie on the floor with your knees bent about 90 degrees and arms crossed on your chest. As a warm-up to the crunch, press the small of your back into the floor by squeezing your abs and thrusting your hips forward. Hold this position for a count of six, and do ten repetitions. To perform the crunch, raise just your shoulders off the floor, leading with your chest, not your head. Do as many of these as you can stand, and work up to 100 every day.

waist and let the front of the bike come up to you by bending your arms. Also, keep your weight rearward, with your thighs against the wings of the saddle, to lighten the front tire so your weight is not thrown forward.

1.16

The Crouch: Raise off the saddle by standing on the pedals and balancing on the balls of your feet. Bend your waist and arms, and let your rear end move back until the insides of your thighs touch the rear of the saddle. (*Note:* In the photo to the immediate right, my thighs are actually *behind* the saddle, but because my arms are bent and my body is low, I still have steering control.)

SLOW-SPEED MANEUVERING/ BALANCE

Mountain biking actually requires that you go slow more often than you go fast. Therefore, slow-speed technique is as important as high-speed technique.

At slow speed off-road, many things can bring you to a quick and unexpected stop. In these instances, instinct says, "You've stopped—put your foot down or you'll fall over!" However, if you can balance for a split second and start pedaling again, you can maintain forward progress.

To become comfortable with slow-speed or momentary stoppage, you can practice by first utilizing the general riding position (lowered upper body with relaxed arms) and then pedaling while applying your brakes. Start on a flat area or slight incline, and begin pedaling in an easy gear (middle chainring and big cog). As you pedal, begin applying both brakes lightly so that you are pedaling against the resistance of the brakes. If you feel you are losing balance, just let go of the brakes and pedal.

Note that this braking-while-pedaling technique also comes into play when negotiating technical singletrack, which we'll discuss later.

Once you've gotten comfortable with pedaling while applying the brakes, you can begin coasting while applying the brakes until you come to a complete (or near-complete) stop, then pedal again. The idea is to get comfortable with your

Keeping your body low and your arms bent while going slow improves overall balance and steering maneuverability. (Note that I'm seated.)

slow-speed or stalled balance so that instead of putting your foot down, you pedal the bike forward.

One trick is to backpedal—or "ratchet"—to bring the pedals into a position that allows you to pedal the bike from a stalled position. You can practice ratcheting by pedaling forward on a flat area, then backpedaling a quarter stroke, then forward-pedaling again to propel the bike. This should be done at slow speed, ideally incorporating the braking-while-pedaling technique described earlier.

Once you feel comfortable pedaling at a slow speed in a straight line, you'll need to incorporate turns. Place a marker on the ground around which you can make a tight turn. While seated and keeping the upper body low and arms relaxed, use your braking-while-pedaling technique to approach and round the marker. As you round the marker, look up and find the next place you want to go.

CLIPLESS PEDALS

Clipless pedals work like a miniature ski binding: a cleat attached to the bottom of the shoe pushes into a spring-loaded clamp that holds the cleat to the pedal. To release, you simply twist your foot laterally, the shape of the cleat helping to open the clamp. The benefits are many, including better control of the pedal revolution in technical situations, more efficient power delivery, a more solid connection over bumpy terrain, and not having to look down to locate and engage the pedal.

You've probably heard the horror stories: when you first start using clipless pedals, you'll come to a stop, forget that you're attached to the pedals, and fall down from a standing stop. All I can say is: true. While you may get a few bumps and bruises, the biggest bruise you will suffer from this is to your ego.

Using pedals with no foot-retention device may feel safer because you can get your feet to the ground more quickly, but for general cross-country riding, some kind of mechanism holding your feet in place is actually safer than using nothing. As you ride over rough terrain with no foot retention, it is easy for the feet to move around and even lose contact completely with the pedals. If this happens, you're like a horseback rider on a galloping horse with no stirrups— eventually, you're going to get bucked off. This scenario also makes it possible for your body to slide forward of the saddle, and we all know what comes next. Landing on the top tube with great force is no fun for women or men.

Whether you're using no retention device or toe clips and straps, there is a learning curve. When Shimano first introduced Shimano Pedaling Dynamics (SPD) off-road pedals, beginners and pros alike—yours truly included—fell over like so many dominoes.

As with operating your gears, getting used to the engagement and release of the cleats with the pedals takes time and practice. This is why it's so important to train your muscles' memory before you go out riding with your new pedals—and with other riders.

All of the following exercises should be performed while sitting on the bike. A stationary rear-wheel-mounted trainer is ideal (put a block under the front tire to level the bike), but leaning against a wall or supporting yourself next to a curb works as well. Engage and disengage at least 100 times for each foot, disengaging at the 6 o'clock and 12 o'clock positions of the pedal revolution. Better yet, watch an hour-long television show while engaging and disengaging, the idea being that the motion becomes unconscious.

ENGAGEMENT

The easiest way to engage is with the pedal at the bottom (6 o'clock) of the revolution. Sometimes it's easier to find the pedal with the sole of your shoe at the top (12 o'clock) of the revolution, but the cleat engages more cleanly at the bottom. If you find the cleat–pedal interface at the top of the stroke, backpedal and engage at the bottom of the revolution.

Without looking down at the pedal, tap it with the sole of your foot, listening and feeling for the metal cleat coming into contact with the pedal (putting the metal to the pedal). Next, straighten your leg and point your toes downward slightly

Engagement: Note how the pedal axle lines up with the cleat at the ball of the foot. While you can engage the pedal at the top of the stroke, the cleat will engage more easily at the bottom.

while pushing down with the ball of your foot while pivoting your foot slightly until you hear a solid click. Pull up on the pedal to check if you are locked in.

Engaging at the top of the pedal stroke simply requires a little more ankle force, with the same slight toe point and twisting motion. Several types of pedal systems exist, though, and the feel of engagement may be slightly different.

DISENGAGEMENT

To release, twist your heel outward. From the bottom of the revolution, push down on the ball of your foot while twisting laterally outward, leading with your heel. From the top of the pedal stroke, lift up on your heel and twist your heel outward.

PRACTICE

Once you've engaged and disengaged as recommended, take your bike to a park and ride around on the grass, engaging (and more importantly, disengaging) at the different positions of the revolution.

As you disengage, slide forward off the saddle just before coming to a complete stop, and step wide to the side your foot is coming down to the ground on. Bend your arms and waist, keeping the chest low to the handlebar. This is a more secure way to stop.

When disengaging at the bottom of the stroke, push down with your heel while rotating it outward. When disengaging at the top of the stroke, lift your heel slightly while rotating it.

2 Intermediate Skills

DESCENDING STEEP TERRAIN: USING THE FRONT BRAKE

Many riders are afraid to use the front brake on a steep hill because they fear being pitched over the handlebar. However, as discussed before, if you keep your upper body low and your thighs toward the back of the saddle, your weight won't shift forward as violently.

On most hills, the brakes should be applied relatively evenly. But on really steep hills, you actually need to apply more front brake than rear brake because so much weight is shifting forward, away from the rear brake. In this situation, the front brake has more stopping power than the rear brake. If you don't apply more power to the front brake than the rear brake, then the bike will continue to pick up speed, and eventually the rear tire will begin skidding out of control.

Body position is important for this technique to work. Not only will you lower your upper body deeply downward, at times you will also need to move your thighs past the rear of the saddle so that the fronts of your thighs, not the insides, are touching the saddle. In some instances, you will need to move completely rearward of the saddle. You can practice this on a flat or slightly downhill surface. Gain a little speed and, from your Crouch position (see page 19), bend your waist and arms deeply toward the bike while sliding your weight rearward so that your stomach is over the saddle. Next, touch the saddle with your stomach and come back to the Crouch. The key is to bend your waist and arms enough so that your elbows are still slightly bent and you still have steering maneuverability with your arms.

Next, as you move your weight rearward of the saddle, pull yourself forward and tuck your thighs up underneath the saddle. You can also pinch your knees in so that you are bracing your them against the seatpost. This will give you added stability. Mastering this technique will allow you to go down steep hills without dropping the saddle. Only in the most severe situations should you really need to lower your saddle.

Once you've gotten comfortable with moving your weight rearward, you need to find a hill steep enough that you can practice applying more front brake than rear brake. You can tell it's steep enough if it is difficult to slow the bike down, even with a lot of brake force. As you roll down the hill in your Crouch position, apply both brakes, begin squeezing the front brake with more force, and then release (but still keep the front brake applied) so that you are actually compressing the front suspension under weight transference. The goal is to come to a brief stop, then begin rolling again. Remember to keep your waist and arms bent and your weight rearward.

If you can't find a paved hill steep enough to practice this technique, you can certainly use a dirt hill. But keep in mind that the front and rear tires will lose a little bit of

To control your speed on a steep descent, drop your upper body as far as possible, and even move your weight behind the saddle.

traction. If the rear tire keeps skidding, it is a sign that your upper body is not low enough or your weight is not rearward enough, and you are not applying enough front brake. Make sure that the hill isn't too long and that it has a clear rollout at the bottom.

LETTING GO

When the front tire rolls over a sharp edge while going downhill under braking, it momentarily loses contact with the ground. The tire is basically free-falling for a split second; then, as it comes back into contact with the ground, the regaining of traction causes an abrupt deceleration. The goal when using your brakes (especially the front brake) on a downhill is to let the tires roll over rough spots with little or no brakes, and then brake on the smoother areas where you have more traction.

By letting on and off the brakes, you not only help the bike roll more smoothly and efficiently, you're also using your muscles more efficiently. Keeping your brakes on during the entire downhill will make your muscles fatigue more quickly, and you'll use your arms more to fight the bumps rather than letting the bike roll smoothly with your arms relaxed. A simple test of this theory is to roll off a

curb with a bit of speed. While in your Crouch, roll over a downhill curb with the brakes on slightly until the front tire comes down off the curb. You will feel the bike jerk slightly underneath you. Next, try it without the brakes—you will notice how much more smoothly the bike reacts to the bump. The rule is to time the negotiation of the edge or bump without the front brake on. It's okay to have the rear brake on while negotiating an edge or bump, but the bike will roll even more smoothly if both brakes are off while negotiating the obstacle.

TECHNICAL CLIMBING

Climbing a hill that has poor traction or variances (bumps, ruts, and the like) requires the same basic techniques as in the section on seated climbing, but with a few modifications.

The main thing to remember is to rise off the saddle so that the rear tire is not weighted when it comes into contact with any kind of bump force that reduces momentum.

First, practice rising off the saddle just an inch or so while pedaling. Do not move forward, only upward. (If you move forward and you're on a hill, you run the risk of bringing your weight from over the rear tire and losing traction.) You will do this for only about one pedal revolution. Keep your body low as you would if you were climbing while seated.

Next, place a small log on the ground and practice coming off the saddle as described above, rising off the saddle just as the front tire goes over the bump and not sitting down until the rear tire has rolled onto the log. As soon as the rear tire is on the log, you can sit back down because all you're trying to do is keep the bike's momentum from stopping as the tire hits the bump.

Now, take your log and place it on an incline. As you pedal toward the log,

maintain your seated-climbing position and, as the front tire hits the log, rise off the saddle slightly, keeping your body low and elbows in and arms pulling down. Try to avoid pedaling with a lot of force at the moment the rear tire hits the log; instead, wait for a split second as the tire hits the log, then sit back down and apply power while seated.

For a longer stretch of technical terrain where you need to pedal off the saddle for an extended distance, just remember to keep your weight no farther forward than the nose of the saddle and your upper body low, with arms relaxed and pulling down. Your mantra at this point is "Keep pedaling!"

When negotiating an uphill with larger obstacles, raise off the saddle while maintaining a compact climbing position. Don't move forward of the nose of the saddle.

TECHNICAL DESCENDING

Descending technical terrain uses much of the same technique from the previous section on descending steep terrain. One disadvantage is that the visual stimuli of technical terrain—ruts, rocks, drop-offs—creates more of a panic factor, which is sometimes as difficult to overcome as the terrain itself.

The main difference in negotiating technical descents is that you don't want to put your weight back behind the saddle immediately. Instead, you need to set your body in a position that will let the bike teeter underneath you. Most technical situations find the front tire dropping away quickly with the rear tire following, such as with a rock drop-off or rain rut. If you put your weight too far rearward too early, you run the risk of excessively lightening the front tire and losing traction or control as the rear tire comes down off the obstacle.

You must set your Crouch, keeping the thighs near the rear of the saddle and your body low enough so that as the front tire drops, the saddle—which moves in

Keep your body low as you let the front tire drop away, letting the saddle move through your thighs as it moves forward (see third photo at right). Don't clamp down on the saddle with your thighs.

the same direction and distance as the front tire—moves through your thighs. This keeps your body position balanced vertically so that your weight stays distributed evenly over the bike.

When dropping down a steep face, get into your Crouch position and let the bike roll over the obstacle. Stay relaxed and let the saddle move through your thighs.

POWER WHEELIE

The wheelie—or the act of raising the front tire off the ground, usually to clear an obstacle—is more than just a stunt. While I am in awe of those riders who can pop the front tire off the ground and pedal down the block for hundreds of yards, this type of wheelie is not really useful in trail-riding conditions. Nonetheless, the initial technique of getting the front wheel off the ground is the same.

I also refer to this technique as the "torque wheelie," as it is torque—not arm pull—that initiates the movement to get the front wheel up in the air, followed quickly by a combination of rearward weight shift and arm pull. The goal for trail riding is to get the front tire up just to the level of the obstacle you are trying to wheelie over.

Begin by putting your bike in an easy gear, one that allows you to accelerate easily. Usually the middle chainring and biggest cog works well if you're on a flat surface. (It's actually easier to practice this technique on a slight incline when you're first starting out.) Pedal slowly and get the feel of pushing forcefully down as the pedal comes to the power stroke portion of the revolution. As you "stomp" the pedal, sit up slightly and give just a bit of tug on the handlebar. If the front tire does not come up, you are either going too fast or are in too hard of a gear. Remember, the technique starts with torque and is aided by the upper body shifting up slightly with just a hint

of arm pull. In theory, all you should be doing with your arms is raising them, not pulling. However, in some instances your pedals won't be in the correct position to get the perfect torque, so you may need to use a bit more arm pull to assist the rearward weight shift.

If the obstacle that you are riding over is large enough to arrest the rear wheel's momentum, rise off the saddle slightly as described in the section on technical climbing (page 30) as soon as the front tire is back on the ground, and keep pedaling until the rear tire is on top of the obstacle. As soon as the rear tire is on the obstacle, you can sit back down. In many instances, you simply need to unweight the saddle by raising off by about an inch, just enough to let the tire hit and roll up onto the obstacle without putting any weight on it.

Power wheelie: Raise the front tire off the ground early enough so that it comes down on the obstacle. Rise off the saddle as soon as possible, and stay low so that the rear tire is not weighted when it hits the obstacle. As soon as you've sat down, employ your seated-climbing technique.

CORNERING

As mentioned previously, the best way to initiate a turn is by looking into it, lowering your upper body, and bending your arms to stabilize the bike. Because there are actually three types of turns—flat, off-camber, and banked—there are different ways you need to lean the bike and position your body for the different angles of the surface of the turn.

In addition to keeping your body low, you can also increase your center of gravity by coasting through the turn with the inside foot up (at 12 o'clock) and outside foot down (at 6 o'clock). (The inside of a turn is the direction in which you are turning; for instance, the inside of a left-hand turn is the left side. The outside of a turn is opposite the direction in which you are turning; for example, the outside of a left-hand turn is the right side.) As you begin your turn, straighten the outside leg and put pressure on your outside foot as if you were doing a calf-strengthening exercise. Also, extend the inside knee away from the bike slightly. This will give you added stability.

Remember that you should do your braking before the apex, or middle, of the turn, letting off the brakes at the apex and carrying your momentum out of the turn.

Negative lean: Lean the shoulder into the turn and push the bike upright toward the outside of the turn.

SADDLE-POSITIONING TIP

To further assist in these seated-cornering techniques, it is helpful to be able to move across the top of the saddle and to either side, depending on which way you are leaning. You can practice this by sitting on the bike and supporting yourself against a wall, with both feet on the pedals. With your feet in the 6 o'clock and 12 o'clock positions, rock your hips to either side of the saddle so that it feels like your sit points are moving across and down either side of the saddle. Rock your hips downward toward the foot that is at the 6 o'clock position.

When you're seated normally, your sit points are on the rear wide part of the saddle. When you corner aggressively, they can slide down along the side of the saddle.

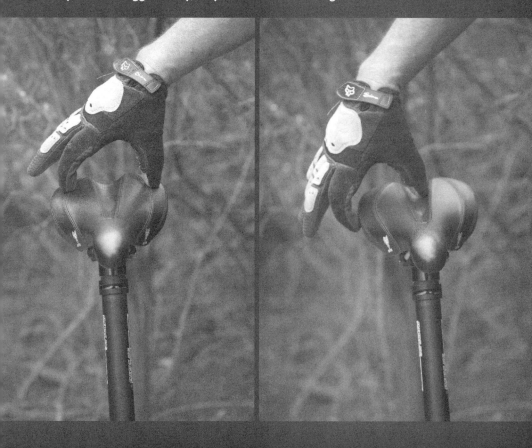

Flat and off-camber turns: To maintain optimum traction on your bike, you should employ what's known as a negative lean. The amount of lean depends on how much the trail's surface angles off-camber, or downward toward the outside of the turn.

A negative lean means you are keeping the bike from leaning into the turn by moving your upper body toward the inside of the bike while pushing the bike toward a more upright position. To do this effectively, it is crucial that you bend your waist and arms and move your upper body so that your head is over your inside hand (see photos on page 36).

If the front tire begins to lose traction while in a turn, keep your upper body low; do not rise up. Rising up will take weight off the front tire and cause the tire to continue to slide. You have a much better chance of the tire regaining traction if you keep your upper body low. If the front tire continues to slide, put your foot out and let it come to the ground (do not reach for the ground with your foot) while maintaining a low upper-body position.

Banked turns: In a banked turn, you lean the bike as it would naturally move toward the inside of the turn. Instead

When you have good traction and/or a banked turn, or berm, with the outside of the turn higher than the inside, you can lean the bike into the turn. Note that you still need to keep your body low so your arms are free to move with the bike.

of trying to push the bike into a more upright position as with a negative lean, you will actually try to force the bike to lean even more by lowering your upper body and moving the handlebar down toward the inside of the turn. Your head will be closer to over your outside hand.

STARTING ON A STEEP HILL

UPHILL

When you come to a stop going up a steep hill, more than likely the bike is in an easy gear. It is next to impossible to get going again by starting off the saddle and pedaling while hopping onto the bike, because the hill will cause the bike to stop before you can get your other foot on the pedal. The trick is to start while seated on the saddle. This technique is easily practiced on a steep street with a curb.

First, you have to get seated. It's easier if you can find something that can act as a step—a rock or the inside edge of the trail—so that you can put your foot on the ground comfortably. Apply both brakes and sit on the saddle, making sure the bike is as close to vertical as possible. Put one foot on the ground and the other on the pedal and position your other foot so that you can get a good push from the power stroke. It is important that you put the foot that is on the ground as close to the pedal as possible, since you need to get it onto the pedal *before* it reaches 12 o'clock. (Here's a tip: while stationary, try tapping the pedal with your support foot and quickly putting it back on the ground.)

Next, assume the seated-climbing position as described on pages 17–19

Starting on a steep hill, footwork: Get the foot that is on the ground up onto the pedal before it gets to 12 o'clock.

Starting on a steep hill, body position: Begin by immediately assuming your seated-hill-climbing position.

(slide forward on the saddle, lower your upper body, arms pulling inward and down). As soon as you're ready to go, release the brakes, push down on the pedal—*do not push off with your support foot*—and immediately bring your support foot up to the pedal and begin pedaling. Don't worry about getting into the toe clip or engaging the clipless pedal; you can do that after you're pedaling smoothly. Remember to pull down on the handlebar as you make your initial pedal stroke and keep pulling down to keep the front tire from popping up off the ground.

DOWNHILL

There are a couple of methods for starting on a steep downhill. One way is to start off the saddle. While straddling the bike, put one foot on a pedal in the 6 o'clock position and the other on the ground. As you begin rolling, straighten the leg that is on the pedal, and step up with your foot like you're doing a calf-raiser exercise; then bend your waist and slide rearward onto the saddle. Next, quickly backpedal the crank (do not pedal forward), get your support foot onto the pedal to get the pedals level, and then immediately get into your Crouch position (see page 19).

Another method is to begin from a seated position (find something to step up onto to help support you). With one foot on a pedal in the 6 o'clock position and the other on the ground, start by keeping your body low, and as you begin rolling, immediately backpedal the crank

(Above and facing page) **To start on a downhill off the saddle, let the bike roll forward underneath you, and get into your Crouch position as soon as possible.**

(do not pedal forward), put your support foot onto the pedal to get the pedals level, and then get into your Crouch position as soon as possible.

When starting on a downhill on the saddle, make sure to keep your body low as the bike rolls forward, and get into your Crouch position as soon as possible.

STOPPING ON A STEEP HILL

Despite being highly effective, crashing is not an acceptable form of stopping on a steep hill. There are techniques for stopping while headed both uphill and down.

UPHILL

If you must stop going up a steep hill (or if you stop suddenly or unexpectedly) and there's not a convenient rock or sidehill to put a foot on, the first thing you should do is apply both brakes firmly. Next, while keeping your upper body low, quickly backpedal the crank into a 6 o'clock and 12 o'clock position, take the foot that is in the 12 o'clock position off the pedal, and pull yourself forward by pulling on the handlebar and stepping down to the ground with that same foot, using a low and wide stance. This will keep you from losing your balance to the side or backward.

Stopping on an uphill: Squeeze both brakes firmly, keep the body low, pull yourself forward, and step wide.

DOWNHILL

If you're on such a steep hill that it's impossible to keep your rear tire from sliding and you can't ride it out, move your weight as far rearward as possible, take one foot off the pedal, and stick your leg out, pushing hard on the other foot to get the rear tire to start sliding out. Steer in the opposite direction of the skid so that the bike begins angling across the face of the hill, letting the foot that is off the pedal come down to the ground. Lean the bike sharply toward the ground, using both tires to dig into the dirt to stop you. Or you may find you can sit down to arrest the slide (man, that's a steep hill!). I've personally found that landing on my rear hurts way less than landing on my head—and I think you'll agree.

Stopping on a steep downhill: With your brakes on and keeping your weight rearward and body low, steer at an angle to the hill and step to the side.

Stopping on a steep downhill, part two: Slide off the back of the saddle while disengaging one pedal and putting your foot down. You will end up completely behind the saddle.

POWER CLIMBING

This technique is used primarily when you have a fair amount of momentum going into a hill, the trail is relatively smooth, and you don't want to change into a lower gear. Use it sparingly, because rising off the saddle while pedaling uses more energy and is less efficient than pedaling while seated. However, it can be very effective for powering up shorter hills when you're moving at a fairly high rate of speed.

As you approach the hill, pay attention to how much the bike is slowing down. Depending on how steep the hill is, you still may need to shift into one or two easier gears. The trick is to time

rising off the saddle to coincide with the point at which your bike begins to lose momentum—rise up too early, and you'll be pedaling too fast into the hill, too late and you'll be fighting the gears.

As you rise off the saddle, ease into the power delivery to get a sense of how hard you should pedal relative to the gear you're in. But don't dally—this has to happen within just a couple of pedal strokes. You then need to bear down on the pedals with force, using a pulling motion on the handlebar that is rearward, slightly downward, and also side to side. As one pedal comes around, pull with the corresponding arm as though you were trying to pull one side of the handlebar

upward and across the midline of the bike. Keep your upper body relatively low, and try not to bounce vertically as your legs go up and down. You should be fairly close to the seat, as this will minimize the vertical oscillation of the legs and keep the suspension from compressing too much with each pedal stroke. This is important because vertical oscillation, combined with suspension compression, can remove weight from the rear tire, which in turn can cause a loss of traction and tire spin. Also be careful not to move too far forward in front of the saddle, as this will take weight off the rear tire and loss of traction may occur. A good rule of thumb is to be able to feel the nose of the saddle grazing the backs of your thighs on each pedal stroke.

Rise off the saddle as the hill begins to increase, staying low and rocking the bike side to side as you pull on the handlebar.

3 Advanced Skills

ADVANCED BRAKING

As I mentioned earlier, there are few instances when you shouldn't use both brakes at the same time. There is a technique, however, that lets you change the line of the bike more quickly rather than just following the radius of the turn. This technique can also help you avoid the front tire washing out, as it can redirect the front tire by turning it in the direction of a controlled rear-tire skid. The technique makes the front tire go straighter and more upright than leaned over. This is similar to the rule of thumb "steer in the direction of the skid"—for example, if the rear tire starts to skid and moves to the right, steer to the right, a technique sometimes called countersteering.

Please remember that skidding should be used only when absolutely necessary, as it causes additional wear on the trail and is in no way a substitute for proper two-brake technique.

The "redirect skid" requires that you understand how a rear tire reacts when locked up under braking. First, you must have enough speed for the rear tire to skid. Second, you have to reposition your body slightly forward to take weight off the rear tire so it skids more easily. Third, you want the rear tire to skid toward the outside of the turn or fishtail to the outside. To get a feel for this, you will need a dirt surface with a slight slope to it, such as a dirt parking lot or wide fire road where skidding will not damage the surface.

The "redirect skid" helps the front tire track a tighter line through a high-speed turn.

As you begin your descent, increase your speed to approximately 10 miles per hour, then establish a Crouch position (see page 19) and apply both brakes firmly so that the rear tire skids. Do this a couple of times, each time applying less power to the front brake so that the distance that the rear tire skids increases each time.

Next, as you begin your descent, sit down, put your left foot in the 6 o'clock position, and straighten that leg as much as possible. Rise slightly off the saddle, or "hover"; apply the brakes; and keep your chest low. As you apply the brakes, slide forward slightly, turn the handlebar to the right, and push down and out with your left foot in the 6 o'clock position.

This should cause the rear tire to fishtail to the left.

Once you get comfortable with the rear tire fishtailing, plot out a curve that you can go around. As you approach the corner, put the outside foot down in the 6 o'clock position and hover as described previously. Keep your body low, lean the bike into the turn, and apply the rear brake to get the rear tire to fishtail. As the tire starts to break loose, let go of the brake quickly. The tire will regain traction and "kick" the bike forward as it hooks up.

Ideally, this technique should be used where there is a berm, or bank, to the outside of the turn. Using this technique on an off-camber turn can cause the rear tire to skid too far off the trail and a loss of control.

As you approach the turn, lean into it slightly and apply both front and rear brakes, then quickly let off the front brake and get the rear tire sliding. (Putting on both brakes at the beginning of the turn helps bias the weight forward slightly.) Countersteer the handlebar until it is pointing in the direction you want the bike to go, then let off the rear brake so the rear tire hooks up. If you examine the lines your tires take during the skid and as the rear tire hooks up, you will notice the front tire tracking inside the line of your rear tire, the rear tire swinging to the outside of the front tire's line.

Putting your foot out in a corner lowers your center of gravity and gives you ballast to countersteer against.

FOOT-OUT CORNERING

The advent of clipless pedals has made foot-out cornering acceptable. Toe clips make foot-out cornering a hassle, as it's not that easy to get your foot back into the clip. Most of us avoid foot-out cornering for that reason. Also, sticking your foot out in a corner used to be a sign of inexperience. Well, actually, it still is, but when used correctly it can help you avoid a crash and aid in traction.

When you enter a corner, there are several things that can indicate the need for putting your foot out (which is different from putting your foot *down*—I'll explain in a minute). One is your speed being higher than expected. Another is an extreme off-camber downhill with loose

rocks where the tires are already slipping even before you begin to turn. The key is to anticipate the move rather than react to the terrain, which means you make a conscious decision to take your foot off the pedal before the turn.

Take your foot off the pedal in a corner using either the seated-cornering technique described on page 17 or in the section on cornering in the previous chapter (page 36). Lead with your heel and point your toe up slightly, with your leg forward of the pedal and straight rather than just dangling off the bike to the inside of the turn. If the bike does start sliding, you want your foot to come to the ground in front of and away from the rear tire, to prevent the rear tire from running over your foot.

Don't reach for the ground with your foot. If the bike starts to slide, your foot's already out there and will come down to the ground naturally. You can practice this by combining the advanced braking technique described in the previous section: when you apply the rear brake, continue applying it until the rear tire slides extremely outward and the bike stops, so that the bike leans over as it stops and you catch yourself with your outstretched foot. Keep your upper

If you need to make an emergency stop during a turn, keep leaning the bike down into the turn and apply both brakes, applying the rear brake more firmly so the rear tire skids. Turn the handlebar in the direction of the skid, and let the bike stop. Your foot will come to the ground.

body low when performing this maneuver, as it will help stabilize the bike.

Another aspect of foot-out cornering is counterbalancing. Putting a foot out helps avoid a possible washout, shifts more weight to the inside of the bike, and increases the center of gravity. When your leg is to the inside of the bike in a turn, its weight pulls downward and inward on the bike. This can help you feel the turn and ground as you go around the corner, because you now have the ability to push on the outside pedal and outside end of the handlebar to gauge how far to lean into or away from the turn. The next time you go around a sharp turn, lower your body, put your outside foot down, stick your inside foot out, and push on your outside foot and hand. You will notice that you can push the bike into a more upright position or let it lean into the turn by lightening up on the outside pressure.

A NOTE ON RUTS Rain ruts running parallel to a trail can be tricky. You have to gauge if your tires will roll through. If not, and if you have enough room and enough speed, a mini–manual wheelie (see next page) is perfect. Make sure you're at a fairly sharp angle to the rut, and do a quick lunge with the front tire, just enough to get it over to the other side. Because you're not going for height, just distance, the combination of lunge, rearward weight shift, and arm pull does not have to be as severe. There are some depressions in the trail, such as a rolling dip where the surface is smooth, and there is a higher lip on the far side of the depression, where it is advantageous to use the manual to get the rear wheel to roll through the dip before the front wheel comes down. You can place the front wheel past the far-side lip and minimize the amount of kick you get from the rear tire. But I caution you to use this maneuver sparingly, as it requires a lot of weight transference that can throw your body off-balance— not the best scenario when on a narrow singletrack with a cliff to one side.

MANUAL WHEELIE

The term *manual* comes from BMX (bicycle motocross) and refers to a wheelie that is performed without torque from the pedals. Instead, you lift the front wheel by shifting your weight rearward and pulling on the handlebar in a rowing motion. When this is done correctly, the front tire stays in the air longer, allowing the tire to carry over obstacles more smoothly while putting you in a balanced position should you need to negotiate other rough terrain. It is also the precursor to doing a manual bunny hop, discussed in the next section.

Most people think you have to pull straight up on the handlebar to get the front tire off the ground. That's one way of doing it, but if you just pull upward, the front tire will come off the ground only a couple of inches. Typically what I see is the rider moving the body over the handlebar and pulling up toward the chest, which puts the body too far forward to control the bike in most situations. Also, this body-forward technique really doesn't work well at relatively high speeds.

To do a manual, you should be carrying a fair amount of speed, approximately 10 miles per hour. You need to lunge the bike forward underneath you, as though you were pushing the bike forward with your arms and feet. Move forward slightly and compress the body; then quickly shove the bike forward underneath you, shifting your weight toward the rear part of the saddle, and as your arms straighten out, pull rearward toward your chest. It takes a little time to get used to, as some riders feel their weight is going rearward too far and they might go over backward. It's very unlikely that this will happen, however.

The easiest way to practice this technique is to start by using a marker on the ground. This is because you ultimately need to time this maneuver over an obstacle. On a slight downhill, place a small stick on the ground as a visual aid, and practice lunging the bike forward and pulling back as the front tire is just a few inches before the marker. The goal is to keep the front tire up in the air until the rear tire hits the marker. For this reason, you are pulling rather forcefully on the handlebar as your weight reaches the rear part of the saddle. Once you've gotten comfortable with the movement and are carrying the front tire until the rear tire hits the marker, start practicing off a curb.

Ideally you will need a downhill slope leading to the curb so you can carry momentum. Start your lunge with the front tire just before the edge of the curb, and make sure your thighs are hitting the back of the saddle as you pull on the handlebar.

Here's the sequence:

1. Neutral Crouch position (body somewhat upright).

2. As you approach the obstacle, move your weight forward slightly (hips approximately at the nose of the saddle).

3. When the tire is just before the obstacle, compress your body, lunge the bike forward with your arms and feet, shift your upper body upward slightly, and pull rearward on the handlebar toward your chest. Continue your rearward pull on the handlebar until the rear tire drops off the curb.

If the front tire is coming down before the rear tire drops off the curb, several issues could be in play. Most likely, you are not forward enough on the bike as you begin your lunge, you're not pulling rearward enough, and/or you're not pushing with your feet (your legs should be relatively straight, like your arms). You have to shift your weight rearward forcefully and quickly enough for the weight shift to affect the bike.

Using the manual for a drop-off: Lunge the bike forward with your arms and feet, and then use a rearward pulling motion so that the rear tire comes down before the front one.

USING THE MANUAL FOR A SHELF

As described previously, the manual is ideal for dropping off a ledge (drop-off) going downhill, the rear tire coming down after the front tire. However, there are some situations when you need to lift the front tire up to a higher level (curb, rock face). Instead of the rear tire hitting the edge of the obstacle first, you need to land the front tire first, then move your weight forward so the rear tire will carry up the shelf without your weight being on the rear tire. In essence, you're using your front tire and handlebar as a leverage point. If the rear tire stalls on the edge of the ledge, begin pedaling immediately, moving your weight slightly rearward and dropping your body lower, or even sitting back down. For taller shelves, you can use a rear-wheel hop as described in the following section on bunny hopping.

Using the manual for a shelf: Lift the front tire just high enough to set it on the upper level. Make sure you're off the saddle as the rear tire hits the lip of the shelf.

BUNNY HOP

This is a useful trail technique for skimming the tires over an obstacle in the trail such as a rut or log, but most people don't know the correct way to perform and employ it.

Performing a classic bunny hop—hopping the bike off the ground while rolling forward—really isn't that difficult. The assumption is that you must pull up the handlebar to get the bike to move vertically. This is partially true, but you actually need to engage a vertical thrust of energy with your legs first, then pull up. It's sort of like doing a standing broad jump while you're on your bike, quickly followed by an upward pull on the handlebar.

Before you can appreciate the motion on the bike, stand on a flat surface, feet shoulder-width apart, waist bent slightly, hands out in front of you at about handlebar level (see photos on facing page). It can help to hold a short pipe or something else that mimics a handlebar. Next, rise up on the balls of your feet, bend your knees slightly, and bounce in place as if you are trying to do little hops into the air. Use both your calves and quads (ankles and knees). As you jump into the air, pull upward on the "handlebar." You can also try pulling your legs up underneath you slightly, as pulling upward on the pedals (using toes clips or clipless pedals) can make hopping the bike easier.

Next, get on your bike, preferably on a slight downhill. Start bouncing on the balls of your feet and springing upward every few seconds to get the feel of the motion. You'll feel the suspension and tires compressing and releasing, and you might even get a little hop out of the rear tire while doing this. (This is actually called a rear-wheel hop and can be used in conjunction with a torque wheelie when needing to get up a ledge.) Next, compress your body into the bike by bending your arms and legs, and try to "jump" upward off the bike while pulling the handlebar up toward your chest, pulling your legs upward at the same time. If both tires don't come up, it's because you're pulling too much on the handlebar and not "jumping" enough.

All this is well and good, but the better bunny hop is one where you raise the front tire first in a manual wheelie (see previous section) then do a rear-wheel hop while the front tire is in the air. This gives you more control, as you don't have to get both tires up in the air at the same time to clear the obstacle. Instead, you raise the front tire to clear, then hop the rear tire as it's coming down.

The sequence is as follows:

1. Manual wheelie

2. Compress legs

3. Jump (explode upward)

4. Push down on the handlebar to get the front tire to come down.

(Right and below) Rear-wheel hop: To get a feel of the hopping motion that will ultimately get the bike off the ground, start coasting and move as if you're jumping off the bike (use your calves to get extra spring). Clipless pedals help with hopping the rear tire off the ground.

(Facing page) The practical application of a rear-wheel hop is getting over an obstacle at slow speed. First, do a seated wheelie to get the front tire over the obstacle, and then immediately put the pedals level, raise off the saddle, and hop the rear tire onto and over the obstacle. You can even lunge the bike forward as the rear tire is up on the obstacle.

The bunny hop shown here is a "wheelie hop," or a combination of a manual wheelie and a bunny hop. The motion starts with a manual wheelie, and just as the front tire is over the obstacle, the compression hop takes place mid-wheelie. Notice how I also shove the bike forward as the rear tire clears the obstacle.

JUMPING

There are several types of jumps—or, rather, there are several types of landings after having come off a jump. All jumps have one thing in common: They kick the bike into the air in a manner that requires the rider to compensate for the reaction of the bike to the jump.

A jump is nothing more than a bump. How big it is, its shape, how much speed you're approaching it with, and the landing area all dictate what you will do to deal with it.

A bike's trajectory off a jump is basically an arc: the front tire rolls up the face of the jump and carries into the air, followed by the rear tire hitting the lip of the face and being kicked up. As the rear tire is being kicked, the front tire is now being forced downward to the ground. If you have enough speed and the face of the jump is steep and long enough, the back tire can get kicked high enough for the trajectory of the bike to be almost directly into the ground. Think of someone

(Above) Downhill angled landing: Because the landing is sloping downhill, it's better to land the front tire first.

(Below) Flat landing: To absorb more impact, I am springing upward and pulling rearward so I can keep the bike in the air long enough to let the rear wheel land first.

diving into a swimming pool off a diving board; his or her arc is such that the body enters the water at almost a 90-degree angle to the surface.

The biggest problem I see with riders trying to jump is tenseness. The bike hits the jump and the rider tenses up, which means that whatever the bike does, the rider does. And because a bike basically reacts to a bump the same way, it is up to the rider to do a few things to get the bike to land properly.

The first thing is to be relaxed and springy. Remember how you got the bike to come off the ground with the bunny hop? It's the same thing with jumping. But instead of using all that vertical energy to get the bike off the ground, the jump is doing the work for you. So all you have to do is make sure you're staying loose. You also have to help the front wheel stay up a little longer, especially if the landing area is considerably lower than the takeoff spot. (Think of the upward pulling motion of the bunny hop.) This is because you want to

Front-tire landing: In this sequence I am establishing a neutral position on the bike as it hits the face of the jump—the bike actually teeters under me as it changes attitude. I then let the bike and rear tire take their natural path (the rear tire kicks and front tire noses down). Note how I am pushing the bike forward in a similar position to that for a drop-off, letting the saddle move through my thighs.

avoid landing the front wheel first in this situation; instead, you want to land the rear wheel first to absorb the impact and spread the impact out from the rear tire to the front tire. For this reason, it is best to avoid landing flat, or on both wheels at the same time. Of course, there are situations when landing the front wheel first (or both tires together) is desirable, such as when the landing is angled downward—for example, when coming off a jump onto a relatively steep downslope. Another example would be if the landing was a "tabletop," where you're jumping from a lower starting point onto an elevated, flat surface.

To get the front tire to stay aloft, you need to shift your weight slightly upward and rearward and use a bit of arm pull. You will need a certain amount of speed and height to achieve this motion, so before going out and doing big jumps, get used to launching off a small jump and feeling the springiness of your legs and arms as you hit the jump and land. As you increase the jump's height, pull back on the handlebar slightly about midway

Rear-tire landing: In contrast with the front-tire landing technique, I am leaning back and pulling rearward slightly at the lip of the jump so the rear tire will land before the front one.

through the jump, and see if you can get the rear tire to hit before the front tire. It's not going to happen by itself—you have to help it a little.

Remember the earlier diving analogy? Divers use the diving board to spring into the air; as they are in the air, they are moving their upper bodies forward so that their trajectories will allow them to enter the water with their hands first. Now let's say you wanted to do a cannonball or land feet first. You would bounce on the board, but instead of leaning forward, you would keep your body upright. It takes a little body control, but you're basically using the spring of the board to help you.

If you want to land the front tire first, you need to employ the technique of keeping your body low while letting the saddle move through your thighs, as discussed in the section on technical descending. As the bike gets air, go with the bike's natural trajectory, letting the front tire drop first while the back tire comes up. Remember to stay loose and let the saddle move through and forward of your thighs; otherwise, the saddle will kick your body too far forward, which means you may land too hard on the front tire and go over the handlebar.

SWITCHBACKS

So much of what we've already covered goes into riding switchbacks: slow-speed balance, sighting the correct line, proper climbing and descending positions, counterbalancing, and braking. If you're like most people (or even seasoned riders), the switchback, especially down-hill, can be one of the most daunting things you can attempt because you're not only going slow, but gravity is trying to pull you down the hill and the bike is in a compromised position.

UPHILL SWITCHBACKS

As with downhill switchbacks, the line you plot around the turn should angle across the fall line. If you turn too soon, you could wind up going straight up the fall line, which is more difficult and also compromises your rear tire's traction.

To climb a switchback, you must first be in the proper seated-climbing position as discussed on pages 17–19. Start wide on the lower section, and aim for the outside (middle) of the turn. Right before you begin your turn, accelerate quickly, then turn the bike into the turn (middle) and let off the power slightly (but keep

Climbing a switchback requires slow-speed balance, a low body, uphill-climbing technique, and constant focus on looking into the turn.

pedaling) until the front tire is pointing toward the upper section (this avoids the possibility of the rear tire losing traction). As you reach the middle, you might feel the slope of the hill pushing the bike down to the inside. If this is the case, counterbalance your weight to the outside of the turn, pushing the bike as upright as possible and leaning your weight to the inside slightly. Quickly increase power again and look up the trail, not at the sides. It is critical that you keep your upper body low and arms pulling down as you accelerate from the middle to the upper section of trail; otherwise,

the front tire will weave and cause you to lose your line.

If there is a rock or other obstacle in the middle section of the switchback, be aware that you may need to rise off the saddle briefly to let the rear tire roll up and over the obstacle.

Finishing an uphill switchback: Keep your body low and your head looking into the turn and up the trail. Notice how far forward on the saddle I am, keeping the weight balanced in the middle of the bike.

DOWNHILL SWITCHBACKS

The best thing you can do to practice the proper techniques for riding downhill switchbacks before actually tackling them is to become proficient at the on–off braking technique on a steep hill, as discussed in the section on using the front brake while descending steep terrain. You will need to be able to come to an almost complete stop, let go quickly, and then apply the brakes again—sometimes several times during the turn—while the bike's front tire is turned at an extreme angle.

A switchback turn typically cuts a sharp angle across the "fall line" of the hill—the natural line of descent between two points on a slope (appropriate for a switchback because this is where a lot of mountain bikers fall). You can think of a switchback as three parts: the upper, middle, and lower sections. As such, when you approach a switchback (upper), you must take a line that doesn't go into the fall line (middle) too soon, otherwise you will be fighting gravity as you are trying to turn. Start wide (upper) if possible, aim toward the outside of the turn before turning, and then cut a tighter turn across the fall line (middle). This requires a deep Crouch position so that you can turn the handlebar at an

When you're descending a switchback, the lower you can get the better. Note the wide outside line the front wheel is taking in order to cut across the fall line.

extreme angle. You will probably feel as if the bike wants to lean toward the inside of the turn because of the hill's slope. If you do, lean your body toward the outside of the bike/turn, putting pressure on your outside hand. As you creep the bike around the turn with your on–off braking technique (middle), keep looking down the trail (lower), not at the sides. Once your front tire is pointing down the lower section of trail, the turn is complete, even though the rear part of the bike still might be in the fall line. Stay low and let the bike roll onto the lower section of trail, braking if necessary after the bike is going in a straight line.

A more advanced technique is to sit down and put the outside foot and leg down, keeping the down foot on the pedal as you go around the switchback. However, you still need to position your rear end off the back of the saddle, which requires you to push rearward with the outside foot. You also still need to keep your body low for maneuverability. You can even take your foot off the inside pedal as with the foot-off cornering technique. But once again, keep your chest low for better balance and maneuverability.

If there is an obstacle in the middle of the switchback, it is advisable to use your Crouch position, not your seated position, especially if the obstacle is a drop-off that requires your saddle to move through your thighs as the front tire drops (see the section on technical descending).

PEDAL KICK

The pedal kick is a nifty little trail trick that helps get you down drop-offs that are too tall to roll down, as well as large ditch gaps at slow speed where momentum is not available.

The technique combines a power wheelie (see page 34) with an abbreviated uphill-climbing technique. You have to get the front tire off the ground high enough and long enough so that the rear tire drops off the edge while the front tire is still in the air. You will need to practice the torque wheelie so that you can do a full pedal revolution (pushing once with each foot) in order to achieve and maintain front wheel lift. You will also need to rise off the saddle as soon as the front tire is off the ground so that you are in a ready position for landing off the drop-off.

This technique is best practiced at slow speed, utilizing a curb as your drop-off (the technique is the same no matter if the drop is six inches or six feet). The best gear to practice in is middle chainring and easiest rear cog (2/1; see "Gears by the Numbers," page 13).

Timing is everything with the pedal kick. You can't just roll up to the edge of a drop-off and hope your pedals will be in the correct position. You will need to use your slow-speed-braking technique as well as your pedal-ratcheting technique so you can get your pedals in the proper position as you approach the drop.

As you accelerate and lift the front tire, rise off the saddle, stop pedaling, and get into your Crouch position. If you have achieved the correct front wheel height, the rear tire will drop before the front. If the front and rear drop at the same time, it's not the end of the world, but landing the rear tire first dissipates the impact of the landing more efficiently than landing with both tires at the same time. You'll know you've done it correctly if the rear tire lands first, incorrectly if the front tire comes down first.

A pedal kick drop requires the ability to keep the front tire off the ground long enough for the back tire to drop before the front tire comes down.

Checklists

Mountain Bike Equipment Checklist

Mountain biking requires specialized equipment that makes riding safer and more comfortable. Immediately following is a list of standard equipment that everyone should ride with in addition to a properly adjusted bike (see "Bike Check," page 78).

- *Helmet:* Should be properly fitted; square on head, not tilted back; snug but not tight. Strap-adjustment locks must meet under ears, and the chin strap must be snug. Visor (if included) should not obscure vision. Replace your helmet every five years, as the polystyrene foam breaks down due to exposure to sun and heat; replace immediately if you are involved in a crash. Check the manufacturer's warranty for replacement details.

- *Water:* Drink 8 to 16 ounces for every 30 to 60 minutes of activity, depending on heat and exertion level. The preferred way to carry it is in a backpack with an internal water bladder, also known as a hydration pack.

- *Gloves:* Cycling gloves protect hands from blisters as well as injury in the event of a fall; they also absorb moisture, giving you better control of your bike. Long finger designs offer better protection and grip.

- *Mountain bike shoes:* More rugged than running shoes, these have a solid pedaling platform and a better tread for walking and hiking. Their shape is contoured to adapt to toe clips, and the soles to adapt to clipless-pedal cleats.

- *Shorts:* Cycling-specific shorts with their special liner absorb perspiration, reduce chafing, and have a contoured fit that won't get in the way of the saddle.

- *Upper-body clothing:* Choose close-fitting, wicking material that helps perspiration evaporate. Avoid baggy cotton T-shirts or sweatshirts, as they can snag on branches or the bike's saddle; plus, cotton stays wet and can contribute to hypothermia in extreme cases. For cooler weather, dress in layers, and always carry a windbreaker.

• *Protective eye wear (such as sport shields):* Guards against branches, bugs, and dust.

• *Tools:* Carry a minimum of a tire lever or Quik-Stik, new inner-tube and patch kit, and mini-pump. Good to have in addition: a chain breaker; Allen (hexagonal) keys; pliers or a multitool; an energy-bar wrapper (to use as a boot in case of a tear in a tire sidewall; place the wrapper between the inner tube and sidewall); cash/coins/credit card; and cable (zip) ties.

• *High-carbohydrate snack:* Carry along an energy bar if you plan to ride for more than two hours. If you're fructose- or sucrose-intolerant, try a trail mix consisting of nuts and raisins or other dried fruits such as dried apricots.

• *First aid:* Pack a kit containing gauze, adhesive bandages, antibacterial cream, cloth tape, a bandanna, antiseptic wipes, sting ointment, a space blanket, and the like. Also keep handy your medical info, emergency contacts, identification, and blood type.

• *Sunscreen:* Apply liberally, paying special attention to the neck, ears, and backs of arms and legs.

Bike Check

This list outlines several important aspects of bike maintenance. Because a mountain bike is a machine with parts held in place by retention mechanisms that can become loose, you should always be very sensitive and aware of any loose-feeling components or strange noises that weren't there when you first got your bike. If something is loose or doesn't feel right, don't hesitate to take the bike in for repairs.

- *Cleaning:* Regular cleaning (every two to four rides, depending on exposure to water/mud/dust) can help you spot trouble—such as broken/worn cables and inner wires, bent gears, or frame damage—before it gets serious. Use a low-pressure garden hose or spray bottle to wet the bike, then a soft cloth to clean. (Do not use water at high pressure, as it can damage ball bearings.) Use a biodegradable degreaser on the chain/drivetrain. Take your bike to your dealer as part of your service warranty.

- *Drivetrain lubrication:* Immediately after degreasing, apply a low-viscosity lubricant. Lubricate the chain only, wiping any errant lube from rim-brake surfaces (on cantilever-brake systems).

- *Brake alignment:* Make sure that brake pads do not rub the tire and that they contact the rim surface correctly and completely. (The leading end of the pad should touch the rim surface just slightly before the rest of the pad.) Also, if your bike has disc brakes, make sure that the brake rotors are not rubbing. Never squeeze the brake lever of a disc-equipped bike when the wheel is not installed.

- *Cables/wires:* Check for fraying or unraveling wires and worn, cracked, or broken outer cables.

- *Proper tire pressure:* Should be 30 to 60 pounds per square inch (psi) depending on rider weight. (Rider weight–psi examples: 130 pounds, 35 to 40 psi; 175 pounds, 40 to 50 psi; 200 pounds or more, 50 to 60 psi.) See sidewall for psi-range info.

- *Quick-release position (hubs and seat clamp):* Feel for tension at 90 degrees (halfway closed); close with the palm of your hand, using your fingers to squeeze against the fork or frame. The front hub's lever should be vertical and parallel with the fork blade if possible; the rear lever should be parallel with the chainstay or seatstay. Both front and rear levers can also be pointed horizontally to the rear, as long as they are closed completely.

- *Control-center safety check:* To check for loose stem–handlebar connection and loose headset, do the following: Stand in front of the bike and clamp the front tire between your knees. Grasping the handlebar as you would while riding, hold the front wheel firmly between your knees while turning the handlebar left and right and pushing down on the brake levers. There should be no movement of the stem, handlebar, or brake levers. If anything moves, use the appropriate Allen (hexagonal) wrench to tighten, or take your bike to your dealer immediately.

- *Headset check:* While engaging only the front brake, move the bike horizontally back and forth, and listen for a clicking or clunking sound from the headset area (the steering tube of the frame where the fork and handlebar intersect). If you hear such a sound, take the bike to your dealer immediately.

Glossary

adventure riding See "free-ride."

aerobic Describes activity that increases heart rate and breathing for an extended period of time without putting breathing and heart rate at the maximum level (see "anaerobic").

AheadSet Also known generically as a threadless headset (see "headset"), this is a headset component that uses no threads to secure it to the fork steerer (see "fork steerer"). Instead, it uses a preload cap to set the down force and a threadless stem (see "threadless") that clamps to the fork's steerer to hold the stem in place and keep the headset tight.

air spring In a shock absorber, air is used as the spring medium.

all-mountain Describes a mountain bike that can handle all types of trail-riding conditions (as opposed to a free-ride bike).

alloy A mixture of different metals to produce a new metal with specifically improved characteristics, such as increased tensile strength, greater resistance to corrosion, and the like. An alloy consists of a primary material such as steel, aluminum, or titanium, which is then mixed with smaller amounts of other materials such as vanadium, manganese, chromium, nickel, or boron carbide.

aluminum Used in either bicycle frame tubing or parts, this low-density metal is nearly always alloyed with other materials (see "alloy") for bicycle use. It is lightweight and durable, and it has a high strength-to-weight ratio. When used in frame tubing, aluminum tubes are typically oversized in diameter with thinner wall thicknesses to create acceptable lateral stiffness and light weight. Aluminum can also be formed into sheets to create a monocoque frame (see "monocoque"). When used in bicycle parts, it is either forged or machined (see "forging," "machining"). It is lighter than steel but not as strong due to its modulus-of-elasticity rating.

anaerobic Describes activity that causes heart and breathing rates to reach maximum levels, with the consequent physical exertion causing lactic acid levels in the muscles to rise dramatically in proportion to the workload. Muscular activity that occurs at such an intense rate delivers fuel without the utilization of oxygen.

anaerobic exercise Training technique that increases strength and recovery of the heart by pushing it to its maximum heart rate (MHR) repeatedly. (See "interval training.")

ankling   The action of pulling up with your legs on the upstroke of the pedal revolution.

anodizing   An electrolytic plating process that colors or hardens a thin layer of the top surface of aluminum tubing or parts.

auger (slang)   To travel in a direct path toward the ground at a high rate of speed, displacing quite a bit of dirt with body and/or bike.

ATB   All-terrain bike; a generic term for the mountain bike, but can also be used to describe a city bike or trail bike.

ball burnishing   A process by which small ceramic and/or metal balls are circulated at high speed over a surface to give it a polished appearance. This process also "cold works" the material's outer layer, making the finished product even stronger and more resistant to failure.

bar ends   Also known as climbing extensions, these handles bolt on to the ends of the handlebar to provide additional hand positions as well as a more powerful hand position for climbing hills while raising up out of the saddle.

bail out (slang)   To cut short your ride; to terminate the desired direction of travel before completing a turn, jump, climb, or the like; purposefully disconnecting yourself from the bike before an imminent crash to avoid becoming irrevocably intertwined with it.

bark (slang)   To vomit (synonyms include "toss," "ralph," "Technicolor yawn," "sell Buicks," "lose your lunch," "spew," "hurl").

base   The level of fitness an athlete attains during the early season that establishes long-distance endurance (see "target heart rate").

bead   The portion of a tire that rests inside the box section of a clincher rim and that is pushed outward by the inflated inner tube, then held in place by the hooked lip of the rim's wall. May be either steel or Kevlar.

berm   A banked turn formed by a hillside or other natural terrain, or a human-made bank such as in a dual slalom course.

biff (slang)   Crash.

big air (slang)   The phenomenon of launching your bike so high into the air that you're picked up by local airport radar.

blow up (slang)   What happens shortly after pushing the body to an extreme level of exertion and past the limit at which it can maintain an anaerobic level.

bonding   The joining of two separate components (usually frame-tubing ends) using an adhesive and thermal aging to make a joint or stronger component.

bonking (slang)   What happens when muscles completely run out of fuel (glycogen) after about two hours of heavy exertion; pedaling becomes almost impossible unless it's downhill. Bonking can be mitigated by eating food high in carbohydrates.

boot   A small piece of material that is slipped in between the tire's sidewall and inner tube to temporarily repair a cut or tear in the sidewall.

bottom out   To compress a shock absorber completely under severe load or bump force.

bottom bracket   Primary drivetrain component. Bearing mechanism that rests in the frame's bottom bracket shell and is attached to the right and left crank arms, allowing them to turn.

braking bumps   Small successive bumps leading into a turn or deceleration zone caused by multiple bikes braking through the area.

braze-on   A fixture that has been welded, bonded, riveted, or brazed (soldered) onto the main frame (top tube/down tube/seat tube/head tube) or rear triangle to accommodate accessories such as water-bottle cages, fenders, racks, or cable guides.

bunny hop   A technical bike-handling maneuver that causes both tires of the bike to leave the ground, enabling the rider to jump obstacles such as logs, rocks, or downed riders without slowing the bike.

bushwhack (slang)   To travel off-trail through heavy foliage.

butted   Describes a bicycle frame's tubing whose wall thickness varies across its length. Specifically, the wall thickness is thicker near the weld joint and thinner in the middle. The result is lighter weight, better impact-force distribution, and more material at the weld joint for maximum structural integrity.

cable   The outer sleeve that brake and derailleur control wires run through.

cadence   A given rate of revolutions per minute (rpm) of the crank arms/pedals.

cantilever brake   A simple, effective bicycle-braking system. One brake consists of two vertical arms bridged at their tops by a mechanism (typically a straddle wire), each with a brake pad, or block, attached, facing inward toward the spokes of each wheel. Each arm is mounted to the frame or fork by individual brake studs, or bosses, which the arms pivot on.

carbon-fiber composite   Long, thin strands of carbon that, when combined with a bonding matrix and compaction process, produce a material that is very strong, stiff, and lightweight.

carving (slang)   Also known as "railing," refers to getting into a good turning line and hold it smoothly and forcefully.

cassette   The self-contained cog stack that slides onto a rear hub's freehub body.

center to center   When measuring bike size, refers to measurement from the center of the bottom bracket-spindle to the center of the top tube where it meets the seat tube, in a direct line from the bottom-bracket spindle. (Some bike companies measure their bikes center to top of top tube, or center to top of seat tube.)

chain breaker   Also called a chain tool, it's used for pushing the link pin out of the link in a chain to separate links in order to add or remove links, as well as inserting the link pin back into the link plate to reattach the separated link plates.

chainline   The line plotted between the middle chainring and the middle cog on the cog stack, a line that in theory should be straight.

chainrings   The front gears attached to the right crank arm. (Also called chainwheels.)

chain rollers   The small, round bearings in the links of a chain that allow it to move around the gears.

chain slap (slang)   The noise a chain makes as it comes in contact with the chainstay in rough terrain.

chainstay   The tube of the rear triangle (two tubes on a rigid-rear-end mountain bike) that runs from the bottom-bracket shell to the rear dropouts.

chain suck (slang)   What happens when the lower portion of the chain's links do not release cleanly from the chainring, getting carried up and becoming wedged between the chainring and the chainstay.

cherry picker (slang)   A racer who enters a race in a class below his or her skill and fitness level for the sole purpose of winning.

chromoly   An abbreviation for "chromium–molybdenum." Also abbreviated as "chrome-moly," "cromoly," or "cromo," chromoly is a combination of chromium (a highly corrosion-resistant metal) and molybdenum (a high-quality heavy metal) used in conjunction with carbon and iron to form a steel alloy.

chamois   In the earlier days of cycling, this fine leather liner was sewn into cycling shorts to absorb moisture. It is no longer used, but *chamois* has become a generic description for the synthetic liner found in today's cycling shorts.

cleaning a section (slang)   Making it through a specific section of technical terrain without stopping or putting a foot (or arm, or body) down.

cleat   Can pertain either to extensions from the sole of a shoe that aid in traction while walking in loose dirt (like football cleats) or the component attached to the sole of the shoe that is inserted into the binding mechanism of a clipless pedal.

clipless pedal   A pedal that uses a mechanical retention system whereby the shoe is held in place by inserting a cleat into a binding.

cluster   Older term for the set of cogs (rear gears); also called a cog stack.

cogs   Also called sprockets, a series (stack) of gears located at the right side of the rear wheel's hub. On newer mountain bike drivetrains, cogs are usually configured in stacks of seven, eight, or nine in incremental tooth sizes, while older drivetrains and city bikes usually have five- or six-cog stacks. Each cog represents a different gearing range when used in conjunction with one of the three front chainrings.

coil-over-oil shock   A shock absorber unit that uses a coil spring as its spring medium and a piston that forces oil through internal chambers for compression and rebound damping control. The coil spring is outside the oil chamber, hence "coil-over-oil."

combination tire   Any knobby tire that has a raised center ridge, either staggered knobs or a smooth constant ridge, for use on pavement as well as off-road.

complex carbohydrates   The chemicals in food that the body most effectively metabolizes as fuel for muscles. Found primarily in fruits, green leafy vegetables, potatoes, pasta, legumes (beans), and whole grains (wheat, brown rice).

composite   In cycling terms, the combining of two or more types of materials that are in and of themselves not structural in nature to produce a new structural material. (See "carbon-fiber composite.")

contact patch   The surface area of contact between a tire and the ground at any given time.

control wire   Also known as an inner wire, this consists of the braided wires used to control the brakes and derailleurs.

crater (slang)   To crash ("he cratered").

cooked (slang)   Refers to muscles that are completely exhausted. Other descriptions for this phenomenon are "baked," "fried," or "torched."

countersteering   A steering technique that improves traction and control. The rider puts the inside foot out and pushes the bike to a more upright position while leaning the inside shoulder into the turn to produce a countering effect against the bike leaning into the turn.

crank arm   Comprises primary drivetrain components that pedals and chainrings (right side) are attached to and that attach to the bottom-bracket spindle (axle).

crankset   Comprises crank arms and chainrings.

crash rash   An abrasion caused by making contact with the ground while still maintaining forward momentum. Also known as a "strawberry."

cross-country (XC)   General trail riding with no extremely technical terrain.

cross-up   Aerial maneuver that involves turning the handlebar/front wheel while in the air. Used to change the direction of the front end, or trajectory of the bike when combined with body English.

crotch clearance   Also known as "stand-over height," the amount of clearance between the top tube of the bike and the top of the inseam while straddling a bike flat-footed over the middle of the top tube.

dab (slang)   Generally speaking, to take your foot or hand off the bike and touch it to a fixed point (ground, tree) to maintain your balance. In Observed Trials competition, it pertains specifically to a scoring penalty when this action occurs.

damping   An internal mechanism that controls the speed of a shock absorber's compression and/or rebound.

derailleur   Primary drivetrain component that moves the chain from one chainring or cog to the next.

disc brake   A brake that uses a rotor and either mechanically or hydraulically operated pads in a self-contained unit. (Mechanical disc brakes use a control wire.)

double jump   A terrain surface producing a jump that has two bumps with a valley in the middle.

doubletrack   A narrow, unimproved vehicle dirt road that has parallel tire grooves.

double-wall rim   Also known as a box-section rim, this rim uses two walls for the spoke-nipple area, creating a box-shaped cross section. Stronger than a single-wall rim.

down tube   The lower tube on a bicycle frame's front triangle that connects the head tube and bottom bracket.

downshift   Shifting the gears from a higher to a lower, or easier, gear.

drivetrain   The crankset, bottom bracket, cogs, chain, pedals, and derailleurs.

drop-off   A sharp difference in terrain where the lower section drops away steeply from the upper section, much like a stairstep. Usually used to describe a downhill section of terrain.

dropout   The parts in a frame where the axles of the hubs reside.

dual suspension   Any bike that has front and rear suspension units.

effective top-tube length   On mountain bikes that use a sloping top tube (see "sloping top tube"), the measurement of the top tube if it were measured on a horizontal plane between the head tube and the theoretical meeting point of the seat tube.

elastomer   Used primarily in suspension systems as the spring medium, this is a plastic material that is cast.

endo   From "end over end," when the rear end of the bike comes up with the front wheel still on the ground to the point that it propels the rider over the handlebar.

epic   Monumentally long, arduous ride where participants usually run out of food and water well before the end and go through a range of emotions, from ecstasy to misery to wanting to kill whoever thought of the ride in the first place; a really great ride. Also a ride that has been designated by the International Mountain Bicycle Association as one that is exceptionally beautiful and significant.

etiquette   The commonsense ethic of being courteous to each and every back-country user you encounter. A good rule of thumb is to always approach every corner as if there will be someone coming from the other direction.

face-plant (slang)   A combination of "auger" and "soil sample" whereby in a crash the face is the first thing to come in contact with the ground.

fall line   The direction straight down a hill.

feather   To apply and release the brakes quickly.

fire road   Wide (two-vehicle-width), bulldozed, and packed-dirt road that allows firefighting and ranger vehicles access into the backcountry. Also serves as firebreak. Common in areas with high fire danger.

flip-flop stem   A threadless handlebar stem (see "stem," "threadless headset") with a two-piece handlebar clamp. The clamp allows the handlebar to be removed from the stem and the stem to be flipped over without having to remove the shifting and braking controls to adjust handlebar height.

forging   The formation of a component or part of a component by either pouring material (aluminum, steel) in a molten state into a mold ("melt" or warm forging) and then compressing it or compressing the material in a solid state via a high-pressure press into the desired shape (cold forging).

fork steerer   The tube connected to the fork crown that inserts into the bike's head tube, which also has connected to it the stem and headset (see "threadless," "headset").

fork crown   On either a rigid or suspension fork, the top of the fork just below the head tube where the fork blades (or stanchions on a suspension fork) and steerer meet.

freehub   Primary drivetrain component, a newer version of the freewheel where the freewheeling mechanism (ratchets, pawls) are attached to the hub via an internal bolt, with the cogs sliding onto the body via a splined surface. Allows the hub bearings to mount farther outboard for better load disbursement.

free-ride   From the snowboarding term; used to describe either a type of mountain bike with longer travel (up to eight inches; see "travel") for a variety of terrain conditions, up to and including stunts, jumps, and large drop-offs.

freewheel   Configuration in which cogs and ratcheting mechanism are contained as one piece (with removable cogs) that threads onto the hub.

front-center   Distance measured from the center of the bottom-bracket spindle to the center of the front axle.

gear inch   Number that equates to a particular gearing combination on a bike with derailleurs, representing the diameter of a wheel that a 19th-century "high wheeler" bicycle would need in order to cover the same amount of ground with one revolution of the wheel.

geometry   The combinations of vertical and horizontal angles and lengths of tubes that make up the way a frame handles.

gimp (slang)   Injured but not out of commission.

glycogen   The fuel your muscles use for endurance and power. Created by the ingestion of carbohydrates.

gnarly (slang)   Describes terrain or a trail that is technically demanding, rough, fun, scary, or all of the above.

granny gear (slang)   Small chainring, used mainly for climbing. Also known as a pixie gear.

grip shift   Also known as a twist shifter, a grip-style derailleur shifting system consisting of indexed rotating grips located inboard of the handlebar grips.

gruppo (GROOP-oh)   Italian for "group"; refers to the traditional component group (drivetrain, brakes, shifters, and hubs).

gurn (slang)   Also called a digger, this injury is characterized by a chunk of skin or flesh being forcibly removed by a part of the bike or ground during a crash or momentary lapse of coordination.

hammer (slang)   To exert an extreme amount of energy.

hammerhead (slang)   A rider who has only two speeds: fast and faster.

hardtail   A mountain bike lacking rear suspension.

headset   The mechanism housing the bearings; attaches to the fork's steer tube and allows the fork to rotate inside the bike frame's head tube (see below).

head tube   The short section of tubing on the main triangle that houses the fork's steer tube and has connected to it the top and down tubes.

high-tensile steel   A steel alloy that has a high carbon content. Not quite as stiff as chromoly (see "chromoly") and a bit heavier, high-tensile steel requires more material to achieve the same strength qualities.

hitting the wall (slang)   Running out of energy (see "bonking").

hub   The component that allows the wheels to spin and that the spokes are attached to.

huck (slang)   To launch yourself and your bike from a large drop-off.

hybrid   A bicycle that combines the sturdiness, wide gear range, upright riding position, and secure controls of a mountain bike with the speed and reduced rolling resistance of a road bike's narrow tires and wheels. Some hybrids are designed to accommodate wider off-road-style tires, making them adaptable to a greater variety of terrain. A hybrid is not, however, designed to handle severe off-road riding, nor is it able to attain the speeds of a road-racing bike. Also known as a cross bike (not to be confused with a cyclo-cross bike).

IMBA   The International Mountain Bicycling Association, the preeminent mountain bike advocacy organization.

inner wire   The wire coming from either brake or shifter controls that allows the brakes and derailleurs to be operated by the rider.

interval training   Also called anaerobic training (see "anaerobic"), this technique increases strength and recovery of the heart by pushing it to its maximum heart rate (MHR) repeatedly (usually approximately 30 second intervals with MHR being reached at the end of the interval), followed by a controlled recovery period after each MHR period (usually getting the heart back down to around 120 beats per minute for approximately two to three minutes).

JRA (just riding along)   Describes the riding conditions prior to a major failure: "I was JRA on a smooth fire road when my fork snapped."

Kevlar   A synthetic fiber developed by DuPont, it has a tensile strength that is greater than steel, but it's also lighter than steel. It's used in a variety of mountain bike applications, such as tire beads (see "bead"), tire-casing belting (for penetration resistance), saddle covers, and carbon-fiber structural reinforcement.

klunkers   The first mountain bikes, so named because of the sound the conglomeration of parts made during a ride.

knobby   An off-road tire that has a deep, aggressive lugged tread pattern for riding in dirt conditions.

land access   A catch-all phrase that generally refers to the pursuit of gaining or maintaining access for mountain bikers to public backcountry riding areas. Typically used by local, regional, and national volunteer or nonprofit organizations to describe their efforts regarding opening closed trails to bikes, getting newly built trails designated as open to bikes, trail building, maintenance, and the like.

line   The direction of travel through a given turn or section by bike and rider, usually expressed as the desired path of travel: "I had a really good line through that turn."

link pin   The component of a chain that joins the inner and outer link plates and rollers.

link plate   Components on a chain that make up the box section link, held together by link pins. There are inner and outer link plates depending on the section of connected chain. Each link is made up of four link plates, two for the outer link and two for the inner link.

lock up (slang)   To apply so much force to a brake that the tire skids.

loop (slang)   To go over backward on the bike while still holding onto the handlebar ("he looped it"); also a lap of a race course.

Lycra   Brand name for spandex, a synthetic fiber used to produce a wide range of elastic yarns used in woven and knitted fabrics and garments, most notably cycling shorts. Lightweight and breathable, this material can conform to a variety of shapes and has amazing stretch memory, being able to return to its original shape and dimensions after being stretched to up to 600 percent of its surface area.

machining   The formation of a component or part of a component from a billet, or slab of metal, using a milling machine.

main frame   Also called the front triangle, this structure consists of the head tube, down tube, top tube, bottom bracket shell, and seat tube.

maximum heart rate (MHR)   The upper limit at which your heart will beat, which you can also roughly estimate by subtracting your age from 220. A stress test done by trained medical personnel can determine a more accurate MHR.

modulation   The sensitivity with which a biker exerts force upon the brake levers using varying pressure while still maintaining control.

monocoque   A one-piece carbon-fiber main frame, or an aluminum main frame shaped from sheet aluminum rather than tubes.

mountain bike   Also known as an all-terrain bike (ATB), this bike possesses a number of specialized features that enable it to be ridden off-road on dirt roads, paths, and trails, as well as on terrain that the operator would not attempt on anything other than a mountain bike. The specific features include but are not limited to the following: a rugged, sturdy frame that can handle heavy impacts, with rigid or suspension fork and possibly rear suspension; large-air-volume "knobby" tires; an upright handlebar with brake levers and shifter controls on the handlebar within easy reach; a wide-gear-range drivetrain; and powerful cantilever or disc brakes.

mulch (slang)   To completely destroy a component, as in "I just mulched my derailleur."

multiple use   Describes a trail or area that has been designated for use by all kinds of recreational groups (hiking, equestrian, mountain bike). An alternate term is "shared use."

munch   Same as "mulch."

negative lean   A less-aggressive form of countersteering (see "countersteering") in which the rider leans his or her shoulder into the turn while keeping the bike in a more upright position for better traction.

OTB   "Off the back," or left behind by the rest of the pack.

outer cable   Also called cable housing, this is the flexible plastic housing that encloses the inner wires of the brake and derailleur controls.

pace The current speed of an individual or group; as a verb, refers to controlling your energy output during a ride or race.

pedal body The main part of a standard pedal that houses the spindle and bearings. Less expensive pedals have a one-piece molded body and cage.

pedal cage Also called the platform, this is the structure that surrounds and is attached to the pedal body.

peening The process of mushrooming the ends of a chain link pin to assist in retention of the link plates.

pinch flat The result of a tire hitting a sharp obstacle that in turn compresses the tire to the rim, with the inner tube getting pinched and receiving a cut that results in loss of air. When the tire hits the obstacle so hard that two parallel cuts occur from both sides of the rim, the result is called a "snakebite."

point rider The lead rider in a group, or a rider who acts as a scout to inspect terrain and alert other trail users of the group's approach.

portage To dismount and push or carry your bike through a section of terrain.

poser Someone who has the most expensive bike and all the cool accessories but doesn't ride. Also known as a "wannabe," "dweeb," or "Fred."

power stroke The portion of the pedal revolution where power is greatest, from just past the top of the revolution to the bottom.

preload To increase the amount of pressure on a suspension's spring to change the ride characteristics or sag rate (see "sag").

proportional sizing Outfitting in which a bike's parts match the anatomical specifications of the rider—for example, shorter cranks on smaller bikes. One well-known type of proportional sizing is women-specific geometry.

psi Acronym for "pounds per square inch," this refers to the amount of air pressure in a tire's inner tube at any given time. The suggested psi pressure range is typically found on the sidewall of the tire. Lighter riders can run a lower pressure, while heavier riders should run closer to the maximum psi.

pulley wheel   Also called a jockey wheel, this is one of the two gearlike wheels located below the derailleur's pivoting body, which the chain passes over.

pulley-wheel cage   The parallel plates that hold the pulley wheels located below the rear derailleur's pivoting body, which allows the chain's tension to be controlled while in the various gear combinations.

quick release (QR)   This mechanism is used to hold a wheel's hub in the frame or fork's dropouts. It consists of a narrow axle called the skewer, which is threaded at one end to accommodate a nut and is inserted through the hub's hollow axle, and a cam lever at the other that exerts a clamping force onto the dropouts to retain the wheel. A similar device is used on many bikes to hold the seat post in place, making it simple and easy to raise or lower the saddle height.

ratcheting   A pedaling technique that uses partial backpedaling during the pedal stroke to keep the pedals from making contact with obstacles on the ground, or to set the pedals up for optimal power delivery in tight trail conditions.

reach   The distance from the steer tube and handlebar clamp of the stem; the distance between the brake lever and the handlebar grip. More-expensive levers have adjustable reach to accommodate smaller hands.

rebound   The act of the suspension returning to its original position from compression.

resting heart rate (RHR)   Heart rate at complete rest, as in completely relaxed or asleep. Should be taken immediately after waking up while still lying prone.

retro-grouch (slang)   A rider who not only disdains new technology but actually prefers older equipment and frequently complains about the proliferation of technological advancements.

rider compartment   The area consisting of the pedals, saddle, and handlebar.

rim brake   Any brake that generates frictional force for slowing or stopping the rim by mechanically moving brake pads into contact with the braking surface of the rim. Typically a cantilever.

rise   The distance in elevation measured vertically from the steer tube to the handlebar height.

rising rate   A characteristic in a suspension system in which the spring rate gets firmer (slows down) as the compression nears maximum.

rolling resistance   The frictional resistance of a tire's contact patch as it rolls on the ground. The larger the contact patch and/or the lower the tire pressure (psi), the greater the rolling resistance.

rolling terrain   Terrain that is mildly to moderately steep and continually up and down.

roost   From the motocross term "rooster tail," a general term that means either a dirt plume generated by the rear tire, or to go fast (see "shred").

rotational direction   The suggested direction of rotation on a wheel-specific knobby tire (see "wheel-specific tire").

saddle height   The optimum distance of the saddle's height for proper leg extension.

sag   The amount of initial shock travel while at rest when a rider is aboard. Sag allows the affected wheel to rebound and follow terrain more closely.

sandbagger   See "cherry picker."

swag   Free stuff (derived from "stuff we all get"). Sometimes pronounced "schwag."

seat tube   The tube on the main triangle of the frame into which the seat post slides.

seatstay   The two upper tubes of a hardtail frame's rear triangle that connect to the seat tube and rear dropouts.

semislick tire   A tire that uses a smooth or lightly knobbed center section with knobbies at the outer portion of the tread. Not recommended for loose dirt or hard-packed surfaces with rocks or sand.

Shimano Pedaling Dynamics (SPD)   The first modern clipless-pedal system, using a spring-loaded mechanism much the same as a ski binding to hold a cleat that is attached to the bottom of a cycling shoe onto the pedal.

shred (slang)   To master a riding surface or situation.

shuttle   To park one car at the bottom of a hill, take bikes and riders to the top of the hill with another car, ride bikes back down to the first car, and then retrieve the second car with the first.

singletrack   As defined by some public backcountry-management agencies, a trail with a width narrower than 60 inches. Primarily refers to a trail so narrow that there is enough room for only a single user, requiring a single-file line.

sketchy (slang)   Describes a questionable trail condition or riding style.

slick   A completely smooth or lightly grooved tire used primarily for maximizing a mountain bike's efficiency on the road.

slickrock   Most notably found near the southwestern high-desert town of Moab, Utah, this smooth sandstone rock can be a patch surrounded by dirt or the predominant terrain makeup. Primary characteristics are exceptional traction and efficient "dermabrasion."

sloping top tube   A top tube that is lower at the seat tube than at the head tube.

soil sampling (slang)   Similar to augering (see "auger"), this is the act of taking with you a portion of the ground upon which you just landed.

spider   The four- or five-point star of the right crank arm that chainrings are attached to.

spin   Another term for cadence (rpm) that can describe an easy pedal cadence, as in "I'm just going to spin today."

spindle   The bottom-bracket or pedal "axle." On a bottom bracket, the spindle is where the cranks attach and what rolls on bearings inside the bottom bracket shell of the frame. On pedals, the spindle is what attaches to the other end of the crank arms and rolls on bearings inside the pedal body.

split-stop   Cable guide attached to the frame that has a groove down the middle to allow the inner wire and outer cable to be removed from the guide.

spring   The medium that is used to support a suspension system in an open (extended) position; the medium that is primarily responsible for resisting compression forces; also the primary mechanism that rebounds the suspension.

spring rate   The amount of energy needed to compress a suspension's spring from an uncompressed state to one inch of compression, usually expressed in pounds.

sprung weight   All weight, including the rider's, above a suspension mechanism's shock absorber.

squirrelly   Inconsistent, nervous, erratic, or out of control ("a squirrelly riding style").

stand-over height   The amount of clearance between the top tube of the bike and the top of the inseam while straddling the bike flat-footed over the middle of the top tube. Also see "crotch clearance."

stem   The component that connects the handlebar to the fork's steer tube.

stiction   The amount of initial friction a suspension unit possesses before the beginning of the compression stroke and the force it takes to move the suspension. (The word is a combination of *static* and *friction*.)

straight-gauge   Describes tubing that has no wall-thickness variances along its length.

stunt   A human-made trail feature using a variety of natural and manufactured materials to create an alternate line and/or additional challenge.

suspension   Mechanism on the front and/or rear of the bike that helps keep the tires in constant contact with the ground and reduces bump forces transmitted from the ground through the tires.

switchback   A sharp turn incorporated into a road or trail enabling the track to traverse a steep hill.

tabletop   A piece of terrain with a flat-top surface that creates a jump (usually on a dual slalom course); also an aerial maneuver in which the rider gets the bike's frame parallel to the ground while in the air.

tacoed (slang)   Refers to a change in the shape of a wheel's rim after a severe side load due to mechanical failure. Also known as "potato-chipped."

target heart rate (THR)   Used for building the heart's endurance, or base, this is the rate at which a given individual should work at for approximately one to two hours continuously. The basic formula to determine this rate is 220 minus age multiplied by .80 (80 percent of maximum heart rate). Therefore, a 30-year-old person would subtract his or her age from 220 to get 190, then multiply 190 by .80 to get 152, which is the target heart rate. This is simply a guideline for someone exercising for the first time or getting back into shape after a long layoff.

technical   Describes a particularly difficult stretch of terrain, either up or down, that requires a high degree of bike-handling skill.

threadless   Describes a headset that uses a system of a steer tube with no threads to connect the headset to the main frame's head tube. (See "AheadSet.")

TIG (tungsten inert gas) welding   The process of joining various kinds of steel or aluminum tubing together by heating them to a semimolten state with a welding electrode (tungsten) as they are bathed in argon (an inert gas). The gas prevents the weld area from being contaminated by oxygen, which may cause the area to be brittle and weak. TIG welding is less expensive and faster than fillet brazing or lugging and is easier to work with when welding thick-wall frame tubing. Done correctly, it is also lighter and just as strong as brazing or lugging. For these reasons, the vast majority of mountain bike frames are TIG-welded.

titanium   An expensive material that is relatively difficult to work with. It possesses very good tensile strength, modulus of elasticity, and corrosion resistance, and is light in weight, approximately 40 percent less heavy than steel. In mountain bike applications, titanium is used in frames as well as machined and cast parts and components, as well as fasteners. It is typically alloyed with vanadium and aluminum to produce weldability and strength. Frame tubing currently uses a mix of six percent aluminum and four percent vanadium, hence the typical alloy designation "Titanium 6AL/4V."

toe clip   A curved piece of metal (or, more recently, high-impact plastic) that is attached to the front of the pedal and that rises up and over the top of the pedal platform. Attached to the clip and the pedal is a nylon or leather strap that retains the foot across the top and from the front and sides of the shoe. The result is a more secure connection to the pedal for improved power transfer and better grip in rough or wet conditions.

top tube   The upper tube that is connected to the head tube and the seat tube.

travel   In suspension, the amount that a given unit will move to accommodate absorption of a bump force.

unsprung weight   All weight below a suspension system's shock absorber.

upshift   To shift into a higher, or harder, gear. Occurs when increasing speed or descending a hill.

wall   A hillclimb that resembles a near-vertical face.

wash   Refers to the front tire losing traction while turning, causing the tire to slide out from under the bike.

washboard   A series of small (or, in some cases, large) bumps running parallel to the trail, most commonly found at the entrance to a turn where heavy braking occurs.

wheel-specific tire   A knobby tire with directional knobs that improve traction and cornering for the wheel it is intended for (front or rear).

widowmaker   An uphill time-trial on a very steep slope.

Wilderness Area   Land protected by the Wilderness Act of 1964 against man-made intrusions.

About the Author

Mark Langton began mountain biking in 1983 in the Santa Monica Mountains of Southern California. A brief but successful racing career saw him win several local and regional competitions in the Expert class in the mid- to late 1980s. He is a pioneer in Southern California's land-access movement, helping found the Concerned Off-Road Bicyclists Association (CORBA) in 1987 and the Mountain Bike Unit volunteer backcountry patrol in 1988, both of which are still having positive effects in the Santa Monica Mountains National Recreation Area. From 1987 to 1995, he was an editor at *Mountain Biking* magazine, where he wrote dozens of technique articles and covered the best riders in the world. He began teaching mountain bike skills for the Learning Tree University in 1987 and in 1992 started CORBA's Introduction to Mountain Biking Skills class, which he continues to teach today.

Currently special-projects manager for *805 Living* magazine, Mark rides and coaches locally in Thousand Oaks, California, where he lives with his wife, Teresa. For more information about his teaching philosophy, please visit **www.mountainbikeskills.com**.

Mountain Bike! Los Angeles County

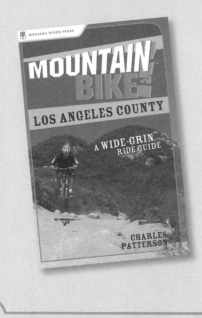

by Charles Patterson
ISBN 13: 978-0-89732-646-9
6x9, paperback, $15.95
224 pages: maps, photographs, index

In this trail guide, you'll find detailed maps of carefully planned routes, some popular and some unknown to many, as well as comprehensive descriptions of what hazards and delights you'll encounter along the way. Los Angeles County has every conceivable type of mountain bike–accessible terrain, from remote, loamy oak-forest-floor singletracks without a person in sight to roller-coaster, rock-garden-filled chutes that will give you plenty of thrills. Several easier routes for novice riders are also included.

Mountain Bike! Orange County

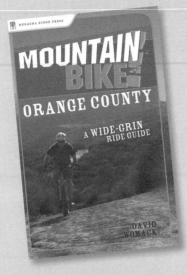

by David Womack
ISBN 13: 978-0-89732-980-4
6x9, paperback, $15.95
240 pages: maps, photographs, index

Mountain Bike! Orange County covers the gamut of mountain biking behind the Orange Curtain. Rip extreme drops in Laguna Canyon, explore the vast reaches of the Cleveland National Forest, and race down suburban singletrack on the Fullerton Loop. Extremely accurate ride maps obtained with GPS technology and produced by cartography experts include ride profiles that give a fast visual of the pleasure and pain that lie ahead.

 MENASHA RIDGE PRESS
www.menasharidge.com

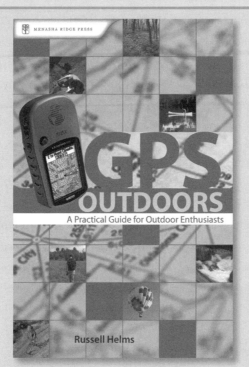

DEAR CUSTOMERS AND FRIENDS,

SUPPORTING YOUR INTEREST IN OUTDOOR ADVENTURE, travel, and an active lifestyle is central to our operations, from the authors we choose to the locations we detail to the way we design our books. Menasha Ridge Press was incorporated in 1982 by a group of veteran outdoorsmen and professional outfitters. For 25 years now, we've specialized in creating books that benefit the outdoors enthusiast.

Almost immediately, Menasha Ridge Press earned a reputation for revolutionizing outdoors- and travel-guidebook publishing. For such activities as canoeing, kayaking, hiking, backpacking, and mountain biking, we established new standards of quality that transformed the whole genre, resulting in outdoor-recreation guides of great sophistication and solid content. Menasha Ridge continues to be outdoor publishing's greatest innovator.

The folks at Menasha Ridge Press are as at home on a white-water river or mountain trail as they are editing a manuscript. The books we build for you are the best they can be, because we're responding to your needs. Plus, we use and depend on them ourselves.

We look forward to seeing you on the river or the trail. If you'd like to contact us directly, join in at www.trekalong.com or visit us at www.menasharidge.com. We thank you for your interest in our books and the natural world around us all.

SAFE TRAVELS,

BOB SEHLINGER
PUBLISHER